THE
Principal
Reboot

THE

Principal Reboot

8 Ways to Revitalize
Your School Leadership

Jen Schwanke

ASCD | Alexandria, Virginia USA

1703 N. Beauregard St. • Alexandria, VA 22311-1714 USA
Phone: 800-933-2723 or 703-578-9600 • Fax: 703-575-5400
Website: www.ascd.org • E-mail: member@ascd.org
Author guidelines: www.ascd.org/write

Ranjit Sidhu, *Executive Director and CEO;* Stefani Roth, *Publisher;* Genny Ostertag, *Director, Content Acquisitions;* Susan Hills, *Senior Acquisitions Editor;* Julie Houtz, *Director, Book Editing & Production;* Miriam Calderone, *Editor;* Judi Connelly, *Senior Art Director;* Thomas Lytle, *Associate Art Director;* Keith Demmons, *Senior Production Designer;* Kelly Marshall, *Interim Manager, Production Services;* Shajuan Martin, *E-Publishing Specialist*

Copyright © 2020 ASCD. All rights reserved. It is illegal to reproduce copies of this work in print or electronic format (including reproductions displayed on a secure intranet or stored in a retrieval system or other electronic storage device from which copies can be made or displayed) without the prior written permission of the publisher. By purchasing only authorized electronic or print editions and not participating in or encouraging piracy of copyrighted materials, you support the rights of authors and publishers. Readers who wish to reproduce or republish excerpts of this work in print or electronic format may do so for a small fee by contacting the Copyright Clearance Center (CCC), 222 Rosewood Dr., Danvers, MA 01923, USA (phone: 978-750-8400; fax: 978-646-8600; web: www.copyright.com). To inquire about site licensing options or any other reuse, contact ASCD Permissions at www.ascd.org/permissions, or permissions@ascd.org, or 703-575-5749. For a list of vendors authorized to license ASCD e-books to institutions, see www.ascd.org/epubs. Send translation inquiries to translations@ascd.org.

ASCD® and ASCD LEARN. TEACH. LEAD.® are registered trademarks of ASCD. All other trademarks contained in this book are the property of, and reserved by, their respective owners, and are used for editorial and informational purposes only. No such use should be construed to imply sponsorship or endorsement of the book by the respective owners.

All web links in this book are correct as of the publication date below but may have become inactive or otherwise modified since that time. If you notice a deactivated or changed link, please e-mail books@ascd.org with the words "Link Update" in the subject line. In your message, please specify the web link, the book title, and the page number on which the link appears.

PAPERBACK ISBN: 978-1-4166-2881-1   ASCD product #121005   n3/20
PDF E-BOOK ISBN: 978-1-4166-2883-5; see Books in Print for other formats.

Quantity discounts are available: e-mail programteam@ascd.org or call 800-933-2723, ext. 5773, or 703-575-5773. For desk copies, go to www.ascd.org/deskcopy.

Library of Congress Cataloging-in-Publication Data

Names: Schwanke, Jen, author.
Title: The principal reboot : 8 ways to revitalize your school leadership / Jen Schwanke.
Description: Alexandria, Virginia USA : ASCD, [2020] | Includes bibliographical references and index. | Summary: "A seasoned principal describes eight key areas in which school leaders can rejuvenate their practice and make their schools the best they can be"– Provided by publisher.
Identifiers: LCCN 2019054226 (print) | LCCN 2019054227 (ebook) | ISBN 9781416628811 (paperback) | ISBN 9781416628835 (pdf)
Subjects: LCSH: School principals. | Educational leadership. | Teacher-principal relationships.
Classification: LCC LB2831.9 .S39 2020 (print) | LCC LB2831.9 (ebook) | DDC 371.2/012–dc23
LC record available at https://lccn.loc.gov/2019054226
LC ebook record available at https://lccn.loc.gov/2019054227

29 28 27 26 25 24 23 22 21 20   1 2 3 4 5 6 7 8 9 10 11 12

THE
Principal Reboot

8 Ways to Revitalize
Your School Leadership

Acknowledgments

It is with gratitude and admiration that I thank the teachers, staff, and leadership of Dublin City Schools for the collegiality, teamwork, mentoring, and friendship. It is a true honor to be a member of this team!

Thank you to my children, Jack and Autumn, for providing perspective, focus, and joy, and to my husband, Jay, for his relentless support and love.

Introduction

When I wrote my first book for principals, *You're the Principal! Now What?*, I was excited to share what I'd learned about making a successful foray into the world of school leadership. Though the book was written for new principals, its intent was broader: I wanted *all* principals to be able to plan and implement their school's systems and structures while becoming more confident in their role. I wanted them to be certain they could lead with excellence and that their students, staff, and school community were in good hands.

In recent months, I found myself speaking to groups of principals who were already secure, experienced, and confident with their leadership abilities but were struggling mightily with how to lead their schools through evolution and change. I began to suspect there was a need for further interaction with principals who were in the midst of their careers but were no longer as inspired and excited about their work as they'd been when they started. *Innovation* was emerging as a buzzword in education, but principals told me over and over that they weren't sure what the word meant in practical terms. What, after all, does innovation actually look like in a system as deeply established as K–12 education? Additionally, and alarmingly, I noticed many principals seemed to be experiencing a decrease in self-efficacy as they moved through their careers, feeling stuck in traditional decision making or hesitant about how to navigate complications related to social media, data, community, and communication.

I understood these challenges because I was facing them myself. The newness of being a principal had long worn off for me, and the constant day-to-day challenges had begun to feel exhausting and overwhelming. I was dismayed to glimpse the beginnings of burn-out in myself, in spite of ongoing self-scoldings and constant self-promises to avoid negativity and lethargy. I was taken aback to find myself victim to the seemingly inevitable pitfalls of the principal-ship: the job requires so much sustained emotional and physical energy that often the only sure way to manage this career is to sit back and let some things go. Give in. Give up?

No way, I thought. I can't let that happen. I wondered, *What if I could rediscover the excitement of those first few years? What if I could find ways to renew my purpose and joy for the job?* What I needed, I decided, was a good old-fashioned reboot.

I began to make conscious efforts to treat every day on the job as though it were my first. I forced myself to audit our school's operations, revisit relationships with others, and reconsider my philosophy on common challenges of the principalship. I took notes along the way so I could catalog and reflect on what made me an effective principal, as opposed to what simply added "noise" to an already noisy job.

This book is meant to provide ideas, inspiration, and support for principals as they navigate school leadership in an ever-changing world. Together, we'll cover eight key areas to reboot your leadership, including rebranding your school with renewed values and mission; reconnecting with your school and community; reinvesting in relationships with students and staff; revamping instructional leadership; reenvisioning teacher leadership; reframing your approach to growth and achievement data; and revisiting your school's operational practices. In the final chapter we'll look at why taking time for yourself to relax, rediscover, and revive can bring you back to the joyful, satisfied, successful principal you aspire to be.

It's a long career. There's no reason it shouldn't also be fruitful and satisfying.

Rebrand: Evaluating and Recommitting to Values and Mission

We've all had that moment when we are working away at a task—alone, with a team of teachers, or with a group of students—and we are struck with this question: What are we even trying to *do* here?

As any principal knows, it is easy to unwittingly lose focus and purpose—within ourselves, certainly, but also with our entire school community. We may assume we are moving in the right direction, because we are assiduously setting goals and creating improvement plans, but we can't be sure. There's no real way to know—not without an end point to guide us.

In this chapter, we'll get to that end point by starting at the beginning. We'll first search for areas where we may have lost focus or wandered off track. We'll consider foundational questions about a school's evolution in today's world, investigating key areas such as student behavior and discipline, English language instruction, special education, differentiation, and the school's role as a safe haven for students and families facing trauma, poverty, or mental illness. Next we'll revisit the rationale behind having a solid, well-communicated purpose and consider ideas for auditing, revising, and relaunching a school's mission and philosophy. We'll determine how to communicate those changes in a way that rebrands our school and invigorates a community, thereby reinforcing our influence as a principal, improving culture and morale, and reenergizing the community's core values.

Not long ago, I agreed to team with a principal to plan a professional development session for his staff. Soon after sitting down to plan, we ran into a couple of tough questions about negativity and apathy among his staff members. He stopped, closed his laptop, and put his head in his hands. "I don't know how much longer I can do this," he said.

By *this*, I learned, he meant all of it—leading a school, planning professional development, inspiring a staff. He had lost motivation and a sense of purpose in his work. He could remember a time when he'd been energetic and excited about being a principal, but in recent years his days had lost their shine. Nothing inspired him. In fact, he'd begun to feel resentful. "I'm being paid to solve other people's problems, and where's the fun in that?" he asked. "I'm never the one who *caused* the problems."

"What is your biggest energy drain?" I asked.

His answers tumbled out. He discussed problems with his facility, instructional delivery, community relations, teacher apathy, parent disengagement, and student indifference. His own apathy was a large part of it, too. He was tired of facing the same old thing every day. He had no energy, no fire, no spark or spunk. "I've lost my edge."

"Is there *anything* that still excites you?"

He shrugged. "Not much."

I sensed that we needed to continue this conversation then and there, so I consciously and quietly set aside our original goals for the meeting. The professional development we were planning (on improving communication) seemed secondary when compared with the principal's self-admitted burnout.

"If *you* are feeling this way, it's likely your students, parents, and teachers are, too," I pointed out. I reminded him of the metaphor commonly made about principals and the staff that surround them: if the principal has a cold, everyone has a cold. An attitude of negativity, lethargy, or drudgery can infiltrate every corner of a school and infect all the people in it.

He agreed. "I know it's my job to inspire them by reminding them who we are and what we aspire to be. And I know I'd find some new energy by doing it. But I'm not sure I have the gumption to begin."

"Let's start there," I said.

So we did. We spent our time deciding how we could gauge the focus and engagement of his staff and what we would do if—*when*, we suspected—we found a lack of both.

A few weeks later, his staff was together for the professional development we'd been planning. I opened the meeting with a guiding question: "Can someone start us off by describing your school's mission or purpose?"

No one raised a hand.

"What are your shared values?"

Nothing.

I wasn't asking them about their classrooms, professional goals, standards, instructional approach, or even a school improvement plan submitted to their superintendent or state auditing board. The question was simpler and, simultaneously, more complicated: *What are you about?*

The principal stood, bravely taking the problem on his own shoulders. "I'm not sure anyone in this room, myself included, knows the answer to those two questions. I believe we've fallen into a predictable, comfortable rhythm here at school by relying on the same system of patterns and habits. It may be that we need to revisit our purpose."

It's important to note that there was nothing terribly wrong with the staff's habits and patterns. They just weren't very goal-driven or inspiring—or fun.

They had forgotten their *why*.

Rebranding, Part 1: Why?

In a previous life, I spent a great deal of time in the food service industry. Rarely does a restaurant have a published mission statement. There is no need, really; it is obvious to employees and customers alike: *A restaurant's purpose is to provide a comfortable dining experience, good food, and appropriate experience-to-value. A restaurant should also be financially profitable.* Diners come in, order, eat, enjoy their experience, and walk away feeling that they had a good meal for an appropriate price. Restaurant employees cook the food, deliver it, clean up afterward, and care for the diners; in return, they earn tips and compensation. It is an easily recognizable give-and-take. Mission accomplished.

Schools are more complicated. Each teacher carries a differing philosophy and sense of purpose; some have years of experience, whereas others have mere months. Consequently, a school's teaching staff is the product of a range of college or postgraduate training approaches spanning several decades. Collegial relationships shift with time, as do the philosophies, attitudes, and perspectives of teachers, students, and communities. Complicating the equation are school culture, student demographics, district support, employee compensation, union presence, parental involvement, and special populations. Other complexities are the nuances within various programs that make up a school.

A friend of mine, the principal of a large high school, told me that one of his biggest stressors is athletics. He faces endless issues with coaches, parents, athletes, the collaboration between the athletic department and academic programs, collegiality among high schools in the district, college programs and recruiting, and so on. My friend identifies the problem as a lack of common focus. Some of the sports, buoyed by a few outlier years of exceptionally talented athletes or by traditionally successful teams, are driven to compete for state championships at all costs. Other sports are lucky to field a team at all, much less keep a coach for a couple years running. Athletics, as a whole, exhausts my principal friend. And that is just one department in his school. Add in the responsibility of overseeing marching band, theater, music, student leadership, International

Baccalaureate, Advanced Placement, dual college–high school credit programs, credit recovery, and all the intense programming students need for postsecondary life, and the end product is a gurgling whirlpool of philosophies and purpose.

Principals are hired to lasso all these components together and keep the school moving forward toward the same goal. Sounds simple, but *simple* doesn't mean *easy*. It's teaching students to read, write, and compute while developing habits of collaboration and communication. It's developing the social, emotional, and academic health of all students, in spite of their widely differing backgrounds and abilities. It's preparing to launch students into a postsecondary world, to be responsible citizens in cooperation and harmony with one another. It gets really complicated really quickly, and there is no single formula for doing it.

We can save our sanity by revisiting and reinvesting in the *why* behind our work. We can gather input and insight from teachers and staff so that the *why* stays at the forefront of everyone's mind. Without a *why*, well . . . why, then?

Let's start by pulling off the blinders and reexamining areas that may need attention. A structured way to do this is with a "purpose audit" built around a list of foundational questions to launch conversations—within yourself or with others—about your school's purpose and evolution in today's world.

Conducting a Purpose Audit

Have you ever walked into someone else's house when they are preparing a delicious meal? You say, "That smells wonderful!" In response you get a grateful "It does? Thank you!" Often, the aroma has become so familiar that the host has forgotten it was even there and genuinely appreciates the chance to notice it again. We can do the same with our schools by asking others, "What aren't we seeing or noticing? What might we do differently? What might make us better?" They'll have a different lens and, as such, will be able to see things we may no longer see.

Several years ago, I spoke with a colleague who had been inspired by the television series *Wife Swap*. He had suggested that his superintendent do an "AP Swap," wherein the six middle school assistant principals (APs) in the district would spend a week at another middle school. The superintendent was game and signed off on the project. A team of principals planned and developed criteria, including the time line: there would be two days observing and shadowing, two days immersed as the acting assistant principal, and one day debriefing and communicating ideas with the principal. An additional half-day would be spent with the team of APs discussing what they'd learned and how it had changed their thinking. The program launched to some grumbling and eye-rolling, but as the week went by, minds changed drastically. In the end, the project was unanimously considered a great success. Why? Because the format was such that the APs were free and encouraged to watch, look, listen, and ask questions—of themselves, of the host principal, and of their "home" principal. It opened conversations about why certain operational procedures were in place, which approaches were being used for instruction, and how students were affected by long-standing traditions, decisions, and protocols.

Even if an experiment or experience like this isn't possible in your district, a team approach to inquiry is a great way to reveal some of the blind spots entrenched in your school's routines. The questions driving such inquiry can be asked among supervisors, an administrative team, a committee of teacher leaders, or even the whole staff.

Questions for a Purpose Audit

For the sake of organization, the following suggested questions are grouped according to challenges that schools and principals often face. As you read, think of how you and a team might ask yourselves, "Is this an area driven by focus and mission, or have we lost track of our purpose?" It might be beneficial to focus on just one area—one that particularly affects and interests you, perhaps, or one that causes your staff extra stress and worry.

Student behavior and discipline

- Are you and your staff spending a disproportionate amount of time responding to student behaviors?
- How often, and to what extent, do teachers hold themselves accountable for student behaviors?
- If your school has implemented a positive-behavior program, has it sustained itself over time? Might it benefit from revisiting the original intent of the program or from modernizing the goals and outcomes?
- Do students feel a sense of responsibility for their own decisions and behaviors and those of their peers?
- How tightly are your school's climate and morale tied to discipline processes and procedures?

English language (EL) instruction

- Has EL programming evolved with your school's demographics and enrollment?
- Do you or your teachers have a guiding philosophy and approach to EL instruction? Is it available online for everyone to access?
- What training or professional development has been offered to your school staff?
- Have refugee population issues been addressed?
- Do you have the staffing you need to support EL learners?
- Do EL students feel a sense of belonging at your school? If you're unsure, how might you find out?
- What community partnerships are in place to support families with limited English proficiency?

Special education

- What supports help you, your teachers, and your staff integrate best instructional practices for special education students?
- Does your school's special education program make you proud?

- Do teachers and staff have a solid understanding of the state and federal special education laws?
- Do your school and your district have a self-auditing process to ensure compliance with state and federal mandates?
- How do parents feel about special education services at your school? If you're unsure, how might you find out?

Differentiation

- Educators talk a lot about differentiation in academic settings. In what other ways do you see differentiation in your school?
- As the principal, do you differentiate how you support teachers? Is the differentiation intentional and based on outcome-based decisions, or is it based on favoritism and school politics?
- If you were to poll teachers, how many would feel they have strength in the area of differentiated instruction for students?
- Do your students' parents understand how differentiated instruction works?

Safety

- When you think about your school's safety procedures, what worries you?
- If you surveyed your staff, what would be some areas they identify as weaknesses? Would you agree with them?
- What kinds of supports do you have available to help make smart, sensible decisions about safety procedures?
- Do students understand safety procedures in a developmentally appropriate way?

Trauma and poverty

- Have you or your guidance counselor done research or reading on how to address trauma in the classroom?
- Can you, or a school-based student services team, identify which students are facing traumatic experiences?
- What supports are in place for students whose families are facing poverty?

Mental health

- What authoritative reading, research, or programming have you considered to support teachers and staff who have mental health challenges?
- Have you considered how you are taking care of your own mental health needs?
- Has your school community faced repercussions as a result of troubled students? How did the response affect you?
- Does your community have any available resources you haven't considered to deal with mental health concerns?
- How have your counselors, teachers, and school community addressed the implications of social media/screen time for students?

School function and identity

- Are students safe, happy, and successful?
- By what measures of success does your school define itself?
- Do school visitors feel welcomed?
- Do substitutes feel supported? Do they tend to return again and again?
- Are staff members generally happy and grateful to work in this particular school?
- Are laughter and joy part of the school's fiber?
- Is gratitude evident? Does it outweigh negativity and complaining?

If any of these questions elicited an area of focus for you and your team, you can now home in on actionable steps to address areas of weakness and publicize these plans to others. In the next section, you'll find ways you can rebrand your school by renewing your mission and beliefs and then share this recalibration with your school and community.

Rebranding, Part 2: How?

After we recognize that there is work to be done, it is easy to get stuck in that crippling moment of *how:* "How in the world will we get started?

Where do we even begin to create and implement a philosophy-driven, purposeful plan for our school?"

A couple of decades ago, there was a great push across the United States for districts and schools to create and write mission statements. School leaders diligently assembled committees, held meetings, and created these statements. After the luster wore off, though, many principals found that their mission statements had grown dusty and rusty, stale and buried beneath new mandates, goals, and committees. For some of us, our mission and vision have disappeared altogether, inexplicably absent from our conversations, our planning, and even our websites.

To address shortcomings in yourself and your school, it may be time to dust off those mission statements and recommunicate your overarching purpose. It's a massive undertaking. Many consultants will happily do this work for a healthy fee, and if you're hesitant or unsure of yourself, hiring some help is a great idea. But I'd argue that most principals could lead this work for a staff—*should*, in fact. It takes extensive planning and a fierce commitment to follow-through, but the principal is the person who best knows teachers, staff, students, and the community. The principal has already invested time in observing and absorbing cultural nuances of the building, and the principal also has a vision of what the school can be. Further, unlike the principal, outside consultants may not have the long-term availability required to truly immerse themselves in the building's culture and see the effort through to completion. Principals are there, embedded in the process and in a position to prioritize a recommitment to make the school better than ever.

We recently did just this at my school. To prepare, I did a lot of reading, thinking, and talking with experts. In the end, though, a lot of it came down to instinct, reflection, and a vigilant response to roadblocks. In the rest of this chapter, I'll cover some of the things I learned and some specific tools my staff and I used along the way, and offer suggestions for steps you can take to update and upgrade your school's vision and philosophy.

Launching a Process to Find a New Mission

To be clear, the effort to find and define a new mission could and should take months. Get ready and settle in.

First, *involve stakeholders.* To start, you'll need a committee of focused, hardworking, inspired people to join you. The most obvious members to include are other administrators and teachers (including department leaders, program directors, and special services staff). The committee may also include parents, students, key community members, and district leadership. I found it most helpful to invite any interested individuals through a purposefully vague e-mail asking for volunteers. Those who responded were the type of committee members I needed—if for no other reason than I knew they'd proven that they actually read my e-mails.

There is no denying that involving others through the creation of a committee lengthens and complicates the process of finding and defining a mission. I admit that I was tempted to do an online search for a viable, zippy-sounding phrase and just adopt it as our own. Those shortcuts never work, though. Lifting a mission statement from another school and trying to incorporate it into your school, without input or buy-in from stakeholders, means it will inevitably deflate and disappear. Asking for help in creating an original work means inclusion and empowerment of community members. It means letting others be owners, from conception to conclusion.

Once I had my list of interested participants, I took several weeks to *connect with each of them personally.* I explained the problems with our previous motto and mission statement (a message I would share hundreds of other times during the coming months). I reminded them of our history: since the school had opened decades ago, a culturally insensitive mascot had been abandoned, our district had increased by almost 15,000 students, our student demographics had changed drastically, and our entire approach to student learning had shifted and evolved. Time had diminished and eventually buried any remaining connection to the school's original mission statement. We needed something new that aligned with who we had become—and who we wanted to be.

In talking it through personally, I was able to be certain that each committee member understood our problem and our goal. Every single one confirmed a desire to be part of the work. Next, I sent each member a formal invitation, with pre-established meeting dates and locations, and a very general outline and time line of our goals for each meeting.

With a committee in place, it is time to get to work. Here are some steps you and your committee might follow:

1. Study the current state of being. Consider the following questions:

- Do we have a statement, motto, mission, or vision that defines us?
- Can all teachers, students, and parents articulate what we are all about?
- How have the history and tradition of our school led to where we are now?

2. Decide whether to redefine, rewrite, and relaunch an existing mission statement or start all over. You may be able to dust off your school's previous mission statement and see if it still suits your school. Even if it does still have some applicability, though, you probably won't be able to just skim over it and then post it on a huge banner in front of the building. At the very least, your committee will want to read it closely to see how and where it has value and whether to let it become a maxim your entire school community can readopt as your school's identity.

In our case, we decided to start all over. We wanted to modernize our mission statement and focus it into one comprehensive motto that captured who we are now, what we believe, and what we want to be in the coming years.

As you and your committee review the mission statement, here are some things to consider:

- What history and tradition do we want to honor?
- What are our current demographics?
- Who is our audience?
- Do we all share the same goals? What are they?

- What kind of school do we want to be? One that gives back? One that is welcoming? A school that sings and dances?
- What does success look like for us?
- How can we put these ideas into words?
- When we find the words, how do we want our belief statement to sound? How can it have rhythm and soul, and easily roll off the tongue?

As you answer these questions, it will help to be completely honest and forthcoming with what you grapple with in your school's mission and to encourage your committee members to do the same. Saying something such as "I feel like we're in a mediocrity rut, and I want to find a way out of it" or "I'm seeking some inspiration to capture how awesome we are and can be" will launch much-needed communication and solidarity, especially when others follow suit. Honesty tells the world you're human—but not afraid to lead a movement from "meh" to "magnificent."

3. Send everyone on a research mission. Have committee members get input and ideas from parents, teachers, students, former students, and community members. In our case, we narrowed our focus to one defining question: "How would you describe our school?" We sent out surveys, had conversations with students and key parent groups, gathered feedback from Facebook and Twitter, and even collected student work from teachers who'd made answering the question part of their writing instruction. We kept it simple so as not to limit or influence responses.

4. Summarize and combine. Here is where you might want to outsource a step of the process, if for no other reason than to have an impartial, emotionally detached person help gather the input you receive. Even if you choose to lead this step yourself, the goal is to identify common themes and summarize all the input. In our case, there were thousands of words to sift through, so it took multiple meetings to categorize responses into common themes and come up with five or six sentences summarizing the feedback.

Here's where I urge a little risk taking. Vision and mission statements are notoriously dry and impenetrable. I've read hundreds of them, and they all kind of sound the same, which is a shame, because I know many hours of work and wordsmithing have gone into their development. In this 21st century world, though, why not modernize the language when summarizing the ideas you've gathered? Strive for short and concise, as in these examples:

Instead of . . .		We could write . . .
At Prescott Middle School, we will come together in our quest for excellence so we may prepare students for tomorrow's challenging world.		Excellent today . . . and tomorrow.
At Prescott Middle School, we focus learning and student success through structures of support and continuous improvement in partnership with parents and community.		Prescott: Partnership, purpose, promise.

Or rather than "Making a difference every day," why not be #differencemakers?

5. Find the best wording. I find this the most maddening and frustrating step in any committee's process. When we were going through our mission adoption process, I squirmed under the relentless scrutiny our committee put into deciding the *perfect* combination of words. As a word lover, I knew finding the right words was important—but each challenge felt like a personal affront to all the hours of work we'd put in so far. Yet there we were, hour after hour, arguing the merits of one word over another. "Should we say 'every' student or 'each' student?" "Do we mean 'achieve' or 'accomplish'?" Immersion in the wordsmithing process can feel nitpicky and valueless, but I promise this: it matters. Go ahead and dig deep. Let it happen. Let your committee members argue. The end result will truly represent what your community says about itself.

6. Gather input. Again. Once you have your motto or mission statement somewhat finalized, you can go back to the larger school community to see what they think. You'll want to know if you've missed the mark or if your statements really do encapsulate the values and mission of your school. In our case, we offered our community three viable options and had them vote to choose which statement best described our purpose.

How did we vote? We did it all digitally, through a Facebook poll for our parents and a Google form for our students. Then we gathered all the responses, tallied them up, and had our answer.

A bit of advice that applies to all steps of the process but is particularly relevant at the voting stage is this: try not to take criticism personally. Having led this process for my school, I felt demoralized and deflated to hear criticism of our work. As people voted, I heard grumblings from some who were scrutinizing the process and outcome. I heard fussing and second-guessing. I wept inwardly when one teacher sniffed, "This whole thing just feels very adult-led." We'd gathered *so* much student input and incorporated piles of student responses; the criticism was terribly unfair. It made me want to abandon the whole project. Not a good idea, though. Giving up would be selfish and reactionary. Instead, I stayed the course and, in the end, recognized that the criticism was just another necessary part of the process.

7. Finalize. When the votes are counted and your school's purpose is wrapped up into one solid statement, it will (finally!) be time to put the stamp of approval on it. As the leader, you'll be ready to move forward, even if the outcome is not exactly what you'd envisioned. For me, it was difficult when the votes were in and 74 percent of our school community chose a statement to define us that was not the one I would have chosen. It wasn't about me, though, and I knew it. It was about our community's vision and version of who we were. So I put my wishes aside and got in line with the majority.

Communicating the Results

Creating and agreeing on a common vision doesn't mean the work is done. Next comes the job of sprinkling your mission statement through everything you do. Let's take it beyond the usual steps—adding it to letterhead and putting a banner at the school's main entrance—and think about some unconventional twists. You will want the statement to be a proverbial rooftop shout from every student, teacher, and classroom. Here are a few ways to publicize and advertise your school's new identity with enthusiasm and flair.

Create a new logo to represent your brand. Don't ditch the old one if it is still applicable and well loved. Perhaps it just needs a facelift, or maybe it's time to start all over. In our case, we found a hip, trendy graphic designer who helped create an eye-catching new logo incorporating our belief statement.

Brand, brand, brand. Branding evokes the emotional connection stakeholders have to your school, and it's fun to think of ways you can launch your new logo and vision to the world. You can use Twitter, Facebook, and Instagram, and hashtag it in social media posts. Advertise it. Continuously tell the story of its creation, from idea to life, and ask others to do the same. The key to good branding is consistency of use as well as a genuine emotional connection to the messaging.

Gift it. With the financial support of our PTO, I thanked all the members of our committee with a personal note and a gift showcasing our new logo. All staff members, district leaders, and key student groups received something, too: mugs, pens, shirts, vehicle decals, ID badges, and notebooks. In fact, I am still thinking of new ways to gift our school's vision to others.

Put it to music. With all the words you have on the cutting-room floor from your work developing a mission statement, you'll have a lot of ideas to put into a song. We partnered with the music department of a local university. A professor and some graduate students worked with our students to write poetry and put it into a snazzy, upbeat song. It's just a few verses long, but the chorus ends with our motto. We recorded it and play it before every schoolwide event, assembly, and performance.

Make videos with student voices. People love movies, no? Creating a video (or a series of videos) advertising the "new you" can infuse a lot of fun into the process and the final product. Student voice is important here, whether you work with 5-year-olds or 15-year-olds, because they are fabulous messengers. Our motto was "What begins here will change the world," so we had students videotape themselves declaring, "This is how I am changing the world!" This is something we can do on a regular basis to reflect our current student population. We archive the videos on our school YouTube channel for easy access and review.

Develop and publish a Quality Profile. As a solid representation of your school, your statement can be the foundation for describing everything that's fabulous about the school. Recently, many districts have developed and published a "Quality Profile" in response to an overemphasis on standardized testing that led districts to protest, "We are so much more than test scores!" A Quality Profile allows districts to characterize and summarize the components of educational delivery that may not be captured by traditional data collection practices. These components are typically summarizations and visual depictions of some of the best aspects of districts, including skills and habits the district or school is committed to developing in students; a highlight of arts, athletics, curriculum, student supports, and financially responsible decision making; connections the school has with the community, including ways students and staff "give back" through needs-based service; and celebrations of student accomplishments using a wide and varied definition of "success." If you're looking to boost your school's mission, purpose, and motto with the district or community, creating a Quality Profile is a good path to take.

● ● ●

If you're a principal facing an inspiration crisis, or if you see your school community losing its way, now is the time to right your ship by making a conscious decision to rebrand your school. This chapter included some probing questions to drill into areas of apathy, frustration, or failure. Seeking answers to pointed questions about your school, while doubling down on efforts to address problems, can give you a boost of new energy and focus. Doing so will also reinforce your influence, improve your school's culture and morale, and reenergize your own reasons for being a principal. You'll have a rock-solid answer to the question "What are we trying to do here?"

Reconnect: Finding New Ways to Engage with Your School and Community

In Chapter 1, we considered the benefits of rebranding to invigorate your school and the processes that might help you do so. In this chapter, we will expand that work to think about ways to actively engage in your school and surrounding community.

Let's start with a simple algorithm:

Positive branding and public perception

+

Community support

=

Positive student experience

Now let's add ourselves to the algorithm:

Positive branding and public perception

+

Community support

=

Positive student experience

=

Principal satisfaction

A few years back, I noticed myself sliding. Several times I needed prompts to begin working ahead—most typically on something related to one of our regular school events. My secretary was giving me reminders: "It's about time we sent a communication about . . ." or "Hey, are we still doing the [insert event] again?" *Yes, yes, yes,* I'd say, and scurry to my office to pull out last year's crumpled plans and smooth them into action.

Too often in our role as principals we rely on repetitive patterns in how we communicate and connect with students, staff, and families. Year after year, we follow the same school calendar, host the same community events, and offer the same experiences for students and their families. Our "resting state" becomes reactionary; we address problems as they come to us rather than eliminating them before they start. At that point, when things begin feeling rote and—dare we say it?—boring, or when we aren't preparing for long-standing events with excitement and enthusiasm, it might be time to seek new and refreshing ways to connect with stakeholders.

In this chapter, we'll discuss how to determine which communication practices can be abandoned and replaced by smarter, stronger, and more efficient tools for ongoing, reciprocal communication with students, staff, and families. We'll find ways to tell your school's story, use social media tools, respond to misinformation, and empower teachers to use common communication approaches for celebrating your school's accomplishments. We'll also consider how to engage and reach out to your community in innovative ways. Looking at school-community partnerships through a fresh lens, you can breathe new life into your work.

"Connect with your school community." Principals hear that phrase all the time, yet many of us grapple with how to do so. If we're clinging to communication and outreach practices developed years ago, we may find we've inadvertently increased our workload and the emotional toll of our responsibilities. Further, it's fair to wonder: Who, exactly, *is* the school community these days? How should we "connect"? How do we know when we aren't connecting?

These questions can trip us up, especially because the answers vary depending on the community, the culture of the school, and the ever-changing metric of success, which increasingly relies on unquantifiable factors including social media, political unrest, and a global (and thus easily comparative) world. Many principals know— they've had it drilled into them—that it is important to "build community" in their school. But it's much more difficult to translate that responsibility into action. So, many times, we just *don't*. We lie low, hoping against hope that the stars will align and our days will be uneventful and quiet. We cross our fingers that no one goes rogue on social media with a public rant about our school. We fold into our routines, relying on the same stale systems and programs.

Is this approach safe? Perhaps. Inspirational, invigorating, and sustainable in today's world? Not so much.

Let's start our work in this chapter by clarifying our meaning about school and community.

School and Community: One and the Same

For several years, I have taught a graduate class for aspiring principals titled "School and Community Culture and Relations." The first few times I taught the class, I tried to break it into two distinct parts. The first covered ways to build culture with staff, parents, and students. We talked about building trust, advertising good work, and addressing problems with staff and students. The second part covered how to build community partnerships outside the school walls—specifically, engaging with outside organizations, businesses, and community members that otherwise would not engage with the school.

The problem? Try as I might, I couldn't cut the two parts into clean halves. The community within the school walls and the community outside the school walls can't exist without each other, so they can't be addressed separately. The lines are too blurred. So I stopped trying to separate the two. Now the class takes a comprehensive look at school and community relationships as they truly exist in practical terms. When we talk about a school community, we are referring to students, parents, and teachers who are in the school during the day, and they are all part of a larger community where our students and their families live and work. For principals, it is beneficial to think about the school's roles and expectations and its impact on the larger community, and be mindful of how our leadership can enhance the relationship for everyone involved.

Knowing Your Community

From the onset of public education, schools have often been seen as the hub of an entire community—the reason and anchor for all decisions pertaining to residents. School buildings can be de facto town halls for local community events. Political and social identities of a residential area can manifest themselves in and around the school. The mascot, colors, and motto of the school district are often well known and celebrated with intense loyalty.

This isn't always true, though; in some cases, schools and communities are not so closely tied together, particularly in urban or high-population areas. In some cases, it's a simple matter of demographics. High rates of transiency can affect a school's identity in the community, as can enrollment numbers: when high schools have several thousand students, or when a community has multiple large high schools, the focus on a school's specific programming becomes watered down—not for the students involved in each program, necessarily, but for community members who no longer have a clear connection to or expectation for how they can engage in their local school system.

Regardless of how a school fits into the community—through deep, long-established roots; a distant, peaceful coexistence; or somewhere in between—principals can solidify and enhance their school's role in the larger community by considering how the two can flourish together in mutually productive ways. The answers are as varied as the components affecting them, and it takes some reflection and planning to be thoughtful about the school's role in the community. Let's look at specific ways a principal can proactively and purposefully strengthen these connections.

Reexamining Your School's Programs, Calendar, and Flagship Events

Many schools fall into a rut with the standard, long-running events they host. To remedy the situation, try this: identify an event or a system your school engages in that has you feeling bored or even resentful; then answer these questions:

- How many years has your school hosted this particular event?
- If you're feeling drained or blasé about the event, have you checked in with staff and students to see how they feel?
- Is there a better way to accomplish your goals by changing or refreshing your approach?
- What would happen if you proposed eliminating the activity or replacing it with something else?
- If an event is still beloved by your students and their parents but you are not sure you, as the principal, can endure it one . . . more . . . time, what can you adjust to make it more enjoyable and manageable?

Let's look at a few real-life examples of reexaminations with positive outcomes.

A friend of mine worked in a middle school that had had a football rivalry with another middle school for many years. The schools' principals had encouraged the rivalry because it had initially sparked school spirit and a competitive energy. Yet the two leaders—who held a mutual respect and affection for each other—realized the rivalry may have run its course. Recent redistricting had led to the two schools feeding into the same high school, which made the rivalry divisive and confusing for their students. Recognizing that there was little value in continuing to promote the competition, they took the brave step of canceling their season-ending "rivalry game," as it had long been called, and reorganized the season so the two teams came together in a combined "summer camp" experience, playing with each other in scrimmage-type situations rather than a culminating game. They secured sponsorship from local businesses, which were much more likely to support a positive collaboration and, thus, a larger audience. The rivalry dissipated with virtually no lamenting. On the contrary, there were many relieved parents, athletes, and administrators.

In another example, a colleague in a neighboring state tells about how her high school had, for decades, hosted a Power of the Pen tournament for a state-level writing competition. She had grown to dread it, largely because the only reason it continued was a feeble "Well, we've always done it." In practical terms, the whole tournament was on life support. No one wanted to take on the huge responsibility of hosting the event; it had become a drag for the school's custodial staff; and diminishing numbers in the school's writing club were a symptom of student apathy and disengagement. The burden was falling on the principal to drum up volunteers, support, and energy to sustain the event. She *hated* it. The whole thing.

She was able to find a great solution. She partnered with the public relations office at a small local university, which agreed to take over hosting the event in exchange for the free marketing opportunity it would bring. The university was eager to expand the event beyond what the school had done, because it could handle greater numbers of visitors and competitors and was far better equipped to handle the associated marketing and promotion. The partnership shifted responsibility away from the principal and, ironically, added new energy and excitement to her school's Power of the Pen team. In a few years, the university added a wildly popular debate component. These days, it is much more of a community-based event, a popular weekend-long affair that brings in thousands of people from around the state.

A final example happened to me a few Decembers ago. I was a frantic mess, scrambling to manage all the events, activities, and charities we had planned for our school before the holidays. Everyone around me seemed harried and overwhelmed, too. There were music concerts and performances, assemblies, and multiple charity activities, including a food drive, a "giving tree," and a gift-wrapping event. There was a PTO-hosted pancake breakfast complete with Santa and caroling and a massive cookie exchange. Frazzled and unable to keep up, I was hustling through the teachers' lounge one day when I encountered our PTO president, bent over a box of holiday decorations. I was taken aback to find her in tears. I tried comforting her as she vented about the pressure of overseeing these school events—plus all the things she was managing at home, with her church events, her children, her aging parents, and so on.

I got to thinking. If she was miserable and I was miserable, how were other people feeling? And then, really, *why were we doing this?*

To confirm my suspicions, I asked our school leadership team for some feedback. Their refrain was loud and impossible to disregard: *It's too much. We've lost sight of why we're doing these things and of our purpose as a school.*

Together, we decided we'd do something brave and bold: the next year, we would cancel all school-based events in December. *All* of them.

I wrote an e-mail to our community explaining our rationale. Some events we cancelled altogether; others we simply shifted to less busy times of the year (for example, we moved musical performances to November or February). We urged our families to refocus on their home and family in December, and gave them ideas for how they could engage in holiday charity events in our community. We had exactly zero pushback or protest, and countless responses of gratitude and understanding. With that decision, December went from a dreadful, overwrought time to a pleasant and calm one at school. I, too, relaxed considerably, immeasurably increasing my own effectiveness and professional satisfaction.

Communicating Better and Smarter

Recently I presented to a group of experienced principals about communication practices. Afterward, a member of the audience came up to talk. "When I was a teacher, my principal *never* communicated. The staff knew nothing about important things going on in the school, and our students and parents knew even less. I made a promise to myself that when I became a principal, I'd communicate everything to my community."

And that is exactly what he did. He sent frequent e-mails and held many "stand-up staff meetings," communicating to the staff every time he thought there was something they needed to know. But the effort was wearing him down; he constantly needed to clarify his meaning, intervene in the face of erroneous interpretations of his message, and manage teachers gone rogue with their own interpretations and assumptions. That very week, he'd sent specific details about a visit from local law enforcement personnel related to a student under arrest. The principal e-mailed the staff about exactly what had happened, why the police were called, and what the outcome was. He had the good sense to leave out the student's name, but the staff quickly figured it out, triggering a nonstop litany of chattering and gossip. Then it happened: one teacher forwarded the e-mail to a spouse, who forwarded it to someone else, who posted on a public Facebook page, "In case anyone wondered why there was a police car in front of the school—I got this from my friend. It's an e-mail from the principal." The post included the full text from the e-mail the principal had intended to be read only by his staff.

The principal was despondent, knowing he had compromised a student's privacy, the school's reputation, and the community's sense of trust. "I was just trying to communicate with them so they'd feel 'in the know,'" he told me. "I was careful to share only facts, hoping accurate information would stop the spread of rumors. When I'd been a teacher, I hated being in the dark, but in my efforts to avoid having my teachers feel that way, I made it worse."

I told him what I'd learned from past experience: for principals, sometimes the reaction to our efforts is far worse than the intended action. By adopting a no-matter-what approach to thorough communication, he had created far more work for himself, increased scrutiny from others, and gotten himself in trouble. He was perpetually in reaction mode, trying to clarify and corroborate information, so his intentions were lost along the way.

Together we came up with the following bits of advice:

- *Try to find the sweet spot.* Some principals communicate every teeny-tiny detail with their staff and community.

Others operate in radio silence, only communicating the bare necessities. Although the right approach lies somewhere in between, it is certainly dependent on the tone and expectations of the community, the situation, and the repercussions of giving too much or too little. It is impossible to get it just right every time, but finding the middle ground between "way too much" and "none at all" is a great goal.

- *Never communicate something via e-mail that you don't want forwarded.* This advice might be the best tip in this chapter. If we send something via e-mail, it instantly becomes public record and can be forwarded to anyone, for any reason. The moment it is hurled out into the universe is the moment it is there to stay.

- *Recognize that some things aren't anyone's business.* In the preceding example, the only people who really needed to know about the arrest were the teachers and staff immediately involved. It would have been sufficient to send a simple e-mail saying, "Some of you saw law enforcement vehicles at the building today. Rest assured that everyone is safe, and there is no impact on our school day." It's perfectly acceptable to let staff and community know that you will not communicate information that doesn't affect them. Gossip will fester, despite efforts to avoid it; there is no need for a principal to be part of the process. It's perfectly OK to limit communication when the situation calls for it.

These considerations demonstrate the immense responsibility and the conundrum that come with being a school's communication gatekeeper. It is enough to wear down even the most zealous and vigilant principal. Here are a few other ways to lessen the burden.

Evolve your communication methodology. I once heard a quote that resonated with me both personally and professionally: "Don't cling to a mistake just because you spent a long time making it." There are many ways to find meaning here, but in the realm of communication and the principalship, this tip is a good one, especially if you are investing large amounts of time and energy on the wrong things. It's wise to wonder: *Is there a better way?*

Not long ago, I worked with a principal and his middle school staff on communication practices. Years before, the principal had set the expectation that all teams of teachers would send a weekly newsletter. The teachers understood and embraced his intent—that all parents be fully aware of what was happening at school. Over time, though, they'd grown frustrated. They were pouring huge amounts of time into a weekly newsletter—and *no one was reading it.*

They forged on, because they *believed* in exhaustive communication. Besides, they had an admirable, efficient system they'd used for a long time. Every Wednesday, each teacher on the team wrote a summary of which curricular standards he or she would be covering in class the following week, even specifically naming the standard by strand, theme, and content. The team leader collected and compiled the summaries, then created a beautiful newsletter. It was a lot of information with a lot of words. The team leader made copies and distributed them to students on Friday afternoons. "Please take these home to your parents," she implored. But the majority of the newsletters were still in student binders come Monday, and they accumulated, too, seemingly multiplying overnight. Mid- and end-of-year "notebook cleanout" revealed a semester's worth of unread newsletters.

"Parents don't read them," a teacher lamented on the day we worked together.

"If they *cared* about their child's education, they would," said another. "If only they knew how much important information they miss."

"It's a waste of our time," said yet another. "I don't even know why we do them."

I took a breath and dove in. "Well, why do you?"

Because, they said, they believed parents needed to know specifics of what their children were learning, *and* they wanted parents to know how hard they, the teachers, were working and how laser-focused they were on academic growth. "But they don't care" was the refrain. The room was full of frustration and discouragement.

"I doubt they don't care," I said. "If parents aren't reading the newsletters, and haven't been for years, then perhaps the information isn't as important as you think it is."

The room was silent.

I challenged them further: "What if it isn't an indicator of parent apathy at all, but instead a testament to how much parents trust you?"

That helped cut the tension.

"Perhaps they don't need to know the specific content standards you're covering on any given Tuesday. They figure you've got it covered. They know you're experts and have no need to helicopter or micromanage." Then I added, "But I bet they'd love a quick photo of their kid every now and then. What if you could capture all the time you're pouring into this newsletter and put your efforts elsewhere— in a place it will be received and appreciated?"

The principal took the first courageous step. He announced he would no longer produce long, wordy newsletters every week. Instead, he would communicate with families using photographs and one- or two-sentence updates on his school's messenger system. Teachers followed suit. It didn't take long before written newsletters were a thing of the past, and the school was communicating in smaller, quicker blasts that required little additional teacher time or preparation.

Be a storyteller. Everyone likes a good story. If you are rethinking communication practices, you will gain a lot by shifting away from reporting dry information and toward a form of storytelling. More specifically, try the following techniques:

- Share information that connects to positive emotion—pride, happiness, hope, affection, and warmth.
- Capture students displaying skills or traits to be proud of— collaboration, creativity, patience, kindness, and social and emotional responsibility.
- Use student voices whenever possible; as an example, when promoting an upcoming event, highlight student-produced videos and photos.

- Communicate via pictures; they really are worth a thousand words.
- Avoid long text summaries; people hate slogging through too many unnecessary words.

Use online tools. A paper newsletter is costly in time and resources. Newsletters created with online systems such as S'More, Flipgrid, or Screencastify, sent directly to parents' e-mail inboxes, can achieve communication goals without the time and cost of traditional efforts. Quite honestly, the most effective online tools I've found are Facebook and Twitter. They cost me nothing, and I can constantly push out positive stories, school updates, and schedule information. A common complaint—that not all parents will follow your school (some intentionally, steadfastly avoiding certain social media tools; others unintentionally, innocently missing the memo, so to speak)—is certainly legitimate, but here's a way around it: set up your school website to contain your Twitter feed, and you'll instantly have a way for all parents to access the information. And when the reluctant ones recognize the value of what you're putting out into the world, they may actually choose to sign up.

The bonus to using established communication platforms is the ability to gather data on usage of all these systems to determine who is using each of them and when and how. As an example, my district sees trends indicating we have more female followers on Facebook and more male followers on Twitter; we know we have peak usage at 9 p.m., and we know our community engagement increases as our posts increase. These tidbits help me be thoughtful about how, when, and where we use these tools.

Have everyone use a common communication tool. With new ideas bolstering your school's communication, you might take the brave step of leading your school staff toward a common communication tool. Unfortunately, doing so is more difficult than it sounds. You may have a solid idea of which online tool or app is best, so it's easy to assume it will be a no-brainer for everyone to adopt its use. But a large portion of your staff may disagree—after all, they will be *certain* their favorite tool is far superior.

It might be worth the challenge, though. Why? For one thing, parents hate having different programs and systems to use from one year to the next. Worse, parents with more than one child might have too many places to check for information—too many logins!—which overwhelms them and makes them disengage from the whole thing. Imagine being a parent with three or four children, some in middle or high school, and each child has multiple teachers, all of whom use a different app to provide updates on what's happening at school. The parent could have 10 or more places to check! No wonder they may disengage.

To be clear, suggesting the use of a common tool isn't about micromanaging your teachers and how they handle their classrooms. It is about coming together with one agreed-upon tool, empowering everyone to embrace its use, and together celebrating the satisfaction that comes from being part of a community in which everyone knows what is going on.

Keep it simple. In our efforts to be good communicators, we often get way too wordy. When I write an e-mail, I read it over several times with this in mind: "What can I eliminate? Where am I using too many words?" No one likes to read 100 words when the message can be communicated in 10. I've found it effective to open with bullet points at the top of an e-mail or newsletter, with more detailed information offered after the bullets. The caution, of course, is this: bullet points do have to be short. I've caught myself going into too much detail with my bullets—essentially writing paragraphs and then putting little black dots in front of them. I challenge myself to limit my bullet points to no more than 10 words each.

Remember that nothing replaces face-to-face communication. Although we are discussing how best to evolve in communication practices, evolution doesn't mean abandoning the very best relational tool we have: face-to-face interactions between teachers and community. There needs to be a human element behind what we say and how we say it. That's why it helps to have formal, planned meetings with community members, such as the following:

- Coffee with the principal
- Senior citizen council

- Business advisory council
- Retiree outreach
- Graduate/alumni associations
- Student advisory committee
- PTO executive board
- Community communicator groups
- Teacher advisory council

Social Media: Friend or Foe?

As we know, for better or for worse, principals are constantly sending, receiving, and processing communications. The process seems to grow more complicated as the world increasingly shifts toward being driven by social media. Let's take a moment to dive specifically into this dynamic world of communication and decide how to use it as an advantage rather than let it be a drain on our spirit.

Social media has opened up a nonstop public forum for criticism and commentary. As a result, instead of schools being considered the foundational moral compass for a community, principals might feel their community's compass has somehow turned into an unwatchable, unpredictable mess. In today's world, principals cannot make unilateral decisions without giving careful thought to the repercussions that may erupt from someone's keyboard.

Talk about the fast track to burnout!

A colleague—and dear friend of mine—had long eschewed Facebook and refused to make it part of his school's identity. That's why he was almost upended by one runaway Facebook post. It began on a Saturday and had reached a fever pitch by Monday morning when he walked into his office, innocently unaware.

What happened?

One disgruntled parent posted a question in a community parent group. She made accusations about the school's motivation in its decision to allow production of a student-written play. It's noteworthy that her child had been passed over for a lead role in the performance. Her post made subtle racial implications that initially provoked curious questions but, as the post was shared and commented upon, swiftly began eliciting enraged reactions. Within hours, hundreds of people had weighed in—the majority not even associated with the school. There were comments questioning the school's integrity, the intentions of the theater department, and, of course, the competency of the principal. Rumors were planted and gained traction. A handful of teachers saw the post and tried to refute some of the comments and bring the conversation back toward the reality of the situation, but other posters aggressively attacked their attempts to explain the truth. Several of them texted my friend to warn him what was happening. "It'll die down," he thought.

It didn't. As he pulled into the parking lot Monday morning, he saw the van of a local news station outside the school. His superintendent was calling to ask what in the world was going on. The communications department was calling, too, desperate to develop a damage-control plan. My colleague was stunned: how could one disgruntled parent cause such fervor—especially since her claims were rooted in a personal vendetta and based on inaccuracies? Why would she seek to deface and damage his school's reputation in such an ugly, public way?

The how and why didn't matter. The damage was done. He spent the better part of a week holding individual meetings with parents, students, and his theater staff; responding to countless e-mails and phone calls; and generally living in defense mode as he tried to refute and rephrase some of the misconceptions that had been born from that single Facebook post.

He was demoralized and disconsolate. He seriously considered resigning. He would have, too, if he hadn't taken the time to really narrow his focus down to the core issue, which was this: *how could he gain more control over the message and rhetoric about his school?*

In the end he asked for help, accepted feedback, and took control over the messaging connected to the school. His first step was to stop lamenting the inevitable use of Facebook and instead embrace it as a necessary tool. He started a closed-group Facebook page of his own, with himself and a few trusted staff members as site administrators. Using a feature that required people to request to join the group by answering a series of questions, only members of his school community could join. He posted information frequently and was able to respond to questions posted by community members. If it was a complaint or a question affecting just one person, he clicked "decline" on the post and made direct contact with the poster. When bad information surfaced on a public community group, members of his school community—feeling empowered, knowledgeable, and privy to accurate information—could chime in with the facts, thus helping to manage the dissemination of information.

I've taken the same approach, and I find it hugely helpful. Here are the reasons why:

- *Exclusivity.* The "closed" designation of the group makes people feel they truly have the inside scoop, since "membership" in the group is by acceptance only. They are confident that information is true, accurate, and timely. Are there other groups in which school-related posts can surface, with uninformed comments and judgments? Sure. But our school leadership team "owns" this group, and everyone knows it—so they trust it as a reliable source.

- *Getting a heads-up.* When I am in control of our social media accounts, I have time to think when someone is bent out of shape about something, particularly if it involves a post from an aggrieved parent about his or her child. I call the person and explain that I'm going to decline the post because it may affect only one family, and I ask that we work through the issue together. And if it's a legitimate question that should be posted to the community, I can control when to approve it, which diminishes immediacy and, thus, a poor response. I can read it, reflect on it, and then draft a response giving reasons, rationale, and outcomes. And I get to decide when I'm ready for my explanation to be public.

- *Spreading the work.* Keep in mind, it's not me managing all this. I delegate. One parent requested approval for this post: "Is there a nasty virus going around? My daughter came home sick today with a fever and headache. Anyone else? How long did it last?" This is not something I wanted to approve for our whole community, as it was a question about an individual child's illness and not related to general communication. Further, I feared it would lead to unnecessary online dialogue not related to our school's purpose or role. So I made a quick screenshot of the request, sent it to our nurse, and asked her to call the parent and offer an answer. Later, she told me all the parent really wanted was someone to listen and sympathize. It certainly wasn't something an entire school community needed to think about.

- *Ability to monitor the rhetoric.* I can see and respond when a conversation is erroneous or misguided, so I retain much more influence and keep accountability where it belongs. Of course, this doesn't mean I am constantly watching the Facebook site. Remember, the time line for reading and responding is entirely in my control. My ability to monitor it just helps me be aware of what's being said and who's saying it.

- *Getting the best information.* Members are hearing directly from me—no middleman, no rumors, no nuances. Just straight talk from the principal.

Taking control over school-related messaging is obviously a good idea. Here are a few tips for doing it effectively.

Use what they're using. Although the example I have shared refers to Facebook—and Facebook tends to be wildly popular among adults—the concepts related to control over school-related messaging apply to any tool that gives you a platform for honest, direct, timely information. It could be Facebook, Twitter, Instagram, a website —wherever people can be sure they'll get the straight story.

Share bad news, too. The straight story means you can't push out only the positive. People see right through such an approach, because they *know* challenges and struggles are happening regularly, and they want to know where to go to find information related to difficult things, too. A principal I know used Twitter for up-to-the-minute communication with his community when his school's entire fire alarm system malfunctioned. Students were forced to stand outside in 25-degree weather for almost an hour—without coats— before the local fire department had completed a thorough sweep of the school. The principal kept the community up-to-date with posts about the situation and his consultations with the fire department. His updates were honest and clear and carried no indication of blame or anxiety. He applauded students for their composure and understanding; he reassured parents that their children were safe; he shared general reassurances about the district's investment in a new fire alert system; and he posted pictures of students grinning—shivering, but grinning—and flashing thumbs-ups signs. The situation could have easily incited panic, with parents coming to retrieve their children; instead, it became simply a good story to be told at the dinner table.

Recruit monitors. As mentioned several times, it is exceedingly easy to get deflated and disillusioned by the effect of bad information gone wild. But no principal wants to be on the constant lookout for bad information; frankly, that's more of a spirit-killer than needing to react to the situation. You can avoid this risk by delegating the responsibility to others. I have a few trusted staff members who are happy to be my informal monitors. They send me a text if they have seen or heard something they think requires my attention. They're smart and savvy people, so they don't over-react, but they know when an issue needs my attention. Although they happily volunteer for this important informal leadership role, I reward them with frequent messages of gratitude, by covering a few of their duties throughout the year, and sometimes even by buying them a nice lunch.

Don't succumb to unspoken pressure to respond. Sometimes bad information will find its way to social media and there is nothing you can do to stop it. Often it is so obviously out of line that it requires no response. For example, a friend of mine, the principal of a 3,000-student school, wisely chose to sit on the sidelines and stay silent as a parent's post went awry in all kinds of random and unpredictable ways. The parent had posed a question asking other parents to share their experiences with the district's response to bullying. Hundreds of people weighed in, some with passionate support of the district and some with ranting diatribes against the school and everyone in it. Some turned on one another, so the original post's intent was lost as the replies devolved into expressions of outrage about society as a whole. In the end, the whole thing was indecipherable and required zero action or response. In fact, the comments of the posters spoke volumes by themselves, and the silent majority sat back and rolled their collective eyes. It's OK to choose a no-response approach to these types of situations if you have developed an official place for good information and people know where to find it. There's no need to dive into a swamp where negativity and tantrums live. Keep your dignity and carry on.

Developing Outreach Efforts to the Larger Community

It makes me sad when principals feel that they, or their schools, are detached from their communities. One urban principal described the factors behind his situation: "It's like my school was plopped in the middle of a sea of apartments, and we have no connection to anyone outside our four walls." He was struggling to reach out to a community that was characterized by enormous, boxy apartment buildings, an industrial park amid an ocean of concrete, and limited reasons for reciprocal connections to the community.

Another common version of this disconnection problem happens when a community thinks of the principal as someone they call only when something is wrong. We have all taken phone calls or drop-in meetings from people we've never met until that very moment. Something has gone wrong, they are furious about it, and they have decided that "I'm marching right in to see the principal." We've also taken this negative input from community members who have no investment or emotional tie to our school. Amass a few of those over the course of a week, month, or year, and your morale and hope may dwindle down to nothing. It feels like the principal is a human punching bag, not the innovative agent for change we had hoped we would be.

I have a colleague who was called by a raging business owner. School had been dismissed hours earlier, and she was working late. Two young adults had stolen grocery carts in a crowded parking lot and were harassing drivers by threatening to shove the carts into their moving cars. The owner demanded the principal *do something*. When the principal suggested that the business owner call the police, he sputtered, "But you're the *principal!*" There was no way to know if the perpetrators actually attended her school. Further, her authority had no teeth at that time of day or in that situation. But the business owner could not be convinced otherwise. He hung up in a huff after delivering his parting shot: "I should have known better than to call you. Your school obviously does *nothing* to control these kids."

Is there anything a principal can do to stop being everyone's favorite target in the community? I think so. Here are a few ideas.

Make sure they know you. For many of us, self-marketing is deeply uncomfortable. I, for one, hate it. That doesn't matter, though. I can hate it all I want; it still must be done. And it works. When you show your broader community who you are and advertise the good work you are doing, people feel more drawn to the school and are more likely to support your work.

Embrace video. Video is a great way to bring the goings-on of your school to the broader world. You don't have to be a savvy videographer to create perfectly acceptable videos; even a standard smartphone can capture casual clips to quickly upload and post. Further, programs such as Screencastify or Screenflow can make quality videos seamlessly. Here are a few specific ideas:

- *Start a YouTube channel.* Several years ago, I started a YouTube channel for our school with the intent of posting short videos for our parents with news updates and explanatory information (how parent drop-off and pick-up works, how to sign in your child after an out-of-school appointment, and so on). The channel was well received, so we expanded it to include our student-led video news program. We started creating videos of all sorts of things we wanted to highlight, including seasonal musical performances, events highlighting our diversity and multicultural population, academic achievements and awards, and end-of-year celebrations. Our families can share these videos with family and friends outside our school, which connects grandparents, aunts and uncles, neighbors, and friends to a collective school experience.

- *Create individual staff profiles.* A couple summers ago, I experimented with short staff-profile videos. I did one of my own, titled "Profile of Your Principal," and invited teachers to do the same. We shared personal tidbits about our hobbies and families but also addressed why we love working with students and even foundational beliefs about education. Some of our more shy, reserved teachers preferred to film their video with a colleague or team. You might also consider dispersing this type of outreach over the course of a year, perhaps profiling a different staff member every month, with the goal of sustaining it indefinitely. People love stories about other people, so they'll watch—and grow more acquainted with your school and the people in it.
- *Have fun.* We've all seen social media feeds with principals singing, dancing, rapping, announcing snow days, encouraging reading, or sharing positive messages. For every video that goes viral, there are plenty that don't; but they are still out there, and they are all helping a principal connect a school with its community.

Reach wide. In 2018, there were 327.2 million people living in the United States (U.S. Census Bureau, 2018). That same year, only 56.6 million of those were students enrolled in kindergarten through 12th grade (NCES, 2018). In other words, only 17.3 percent of the U.S. population is enrolled in elementary or secondary school. Of course, each district is different, but if you do some research about your own community, you might be surprised to find that a low percentage of residents have children in your school system. Even in my district, one generally thought of as a community with many school-age children, only 30 percent of households have children attending school. The possibility of your community having a low percentage of children is worth remembering when building your school's identity. It's the reason some principals undertake and find favorable results with a broad outreach effort, including attending popular community events, hosting podcasts or local radio spots, or being involved in community-based social occasions.

Address brand killers. You know what makes a community really mad? A teacher taking to social media to whoop and holler about, say, summer break: "TEN WEEKS OF FREEDOM! Love being a teacher!" Or a snow day: "I LOVE snow days!!!! BACK TO BED FOR ME!!! So #grateful to be a teacher to get these days off! Pajamas all day long!"

When community members see posts like that, while they're heading to their year-round jobs or scrambling to make alternative plans for their children, they get really grumpy really quickly. For reasons big and small, noneducators are poised for resentment when they hear about or see educators having time "off." Even small things like an automated e-mail response saying, "I am on summer break and will not be responding to e-mail. Please try again after August 10," can be received in ways we hadn't intended—as a teacher's disengagement, detachment, or even hostility.

Every time I bring up this issue with educators, most express surprised dismay at how their innocent messages or posts might be perceived, particularly because their intention was simply to share a feeling of excitement. In general, they recognize the damage that can be done by their public celebrations and pledge to do better. If they don't, though, there is very little a principal can do about it; teachers' social media activity is their personal business, and if they choose to use it to damage the positivity associated with your school's brand, you'll have to let it go (and rely on some of the tactics described earlier).

What you can do, of course, is take to social media with a positive message. On a day school is closed, you might tweet on your school account, "Although there is no school today, we look forward to seeing you soon!" If teachers must leave a summer message on their e-mail accounts, you might suggest that they say, simply, "Can't wait to reconnect with you on August 10!" In fact, these occasions can be an opportunity to *enhance* our brand. Recently, our school was closed for a snow day. My husband, an athletic director, tweeted this: "Athletes! Do you have a neighbor who might benefit from a shoveled driveway? Offer to help out and show what we mean by #ShamrockPride!" He got many retweets and expressions of gratitude for this small display of public service.

Meet a need. A friend of mine was the principal of a Title I school in a high-poverty area. Students had limited exposure to literacy resources at home. She used Title I funds to create her own mini-bookmobile and spent one summer night a week driving in a district van, giving books to any and all students she could find. If they returned the book the next week, fine. If not, fine. Soon they came out to greet her as happily as they would if she were driving an ice cream truck. She added music and opened her windows. When she was profiled on the local news, several businesses donated additional monies to continue her mission. I've seen other principals do similar outreach, working alone or with a team of administrators, teachers, or student leaders. The following additional ideas could be adapted to fit a need in virtually any community:

- *Adult community education.* Open the school for a series of classes for community members, taught by teachers or local experts.
- *Trash pick-up.* "Adopt" local streets, waterways, or parks for cleanup.
- *Spring cleanup day.* Host an annual outdoor landscape event to mulch, weed, prune, and plant flowers around the school, hospitals, libraries, or nearby waterways.
- *Supply drive.* Team with local or corporate businesses to provide basic "backpack" essentials.
- *Food pantries.* Communicate with local food banks to determine which food items and supplies are in high demand and host a specific drive for those items.
- *Student role models.* With a student leadership group, develop a "road show" to speak to younger students about positive decision making.
- *Health care.* Partner with a medical professional to support needy children (e.g., providing orthodontic care or dental cleaning).

- *Community resources fair.* Host an evening or a weekend event at which representatives from local social organizations and agencies (e.g., counseling services, municipal services, youth activities such as scouts or recreational sports teams) come to share information with parents.
- *Event volunteers.* Bring a crew to help at a local event (e.g., Lions Club breakfast, parade, festivals, or fairs).
- *"Sister school."* Create bonds with an administrator of a similar school in a different state or country; build partnerships through student writing, online video chats, and community service projects.

Partner with a local business. Developing a reciprocal relationship with businesses near your school—including, for example, a fitness studio, the arts council, a local computer/technology hub, or restaurants and grocery stores—is a great way to build community ties. I've tried with limited success to develop partnerships with corporate businesses, but I find that locally owned businesses are usually thrilled to develop a connection, especially if they get some free marketing out of the deal. At my school, a popular local sandwich shop provides lunch for our staff a couple of times a year and supplies dessert and drinks for our annual student Movie Night. We return the favor by thanking them publicly and profusely in social media posts.

Connect with older and younger residents. A principal friend of mine called the director of a nearby retirement home about a potential visit. That one phone call has evolved into a mutually beneficial partnership based on shared respect and fondness. Students walk to the retirement home for regular visits, and the school makes the elderly residents guests of honor at school events. I've known other schools that have reciprocal relationships with day care centers or preschools that feed into their schools. See Figure 2.1 for a few ideas to launch these partnerships.

Take advantage of seasonal opportunities. City officials and local planners are always eager for extra hands at community events, and such events are a great opportunity to market yourself

---

FIGURE 2.1

**Ideas for Connecting with Older
and Younger Community Members**

Retirement Centers/Assisted Living Facilities	Preschools or Local Day Care Centers
Elementary Schools Can . . . • Bring young students to read with residents and discuss the stories. • Help residents decorate for holidays. • Use conversation starters to share memories. *Middle and High Schools Can . . .* • Bring student artists to the center to do projects or activities with the residents, perhaps for service credit. • Have music or theater students provide concerts or other performances. • Invite teachers to pair students with residents for project-based learning experiences in history, sociology, and social studies classes. • Offer free admission to plays, musicals, games, or matches held at your school or in your district.	*Elementary Schools Can . . .* • Offer parent information sessions on kindergarten readiness. • Offer parents reassurances about school programs and services. *Middle and High Schools Can . . .* • Create a "buddies" program to support students with play-based learning opportunities. • Write and perform a show with students, to be presented at a school open house. • Provide internships for students who hope for summer jobs in camps and as babysitters or, even better, who hope to pursue a career in education. • Set up a seasonal or holiday "shop" for young children to "purchase" presents for loved ones.

---

and your school. March in parades. Show up at memorial events. Light the local Christmas tree. Serve at a concession stand at summer festivals. I admit it—these are things I sometimes dread and wish I could avoid, but I force myself to go, and when I do, it takes me about 10 seconds to remember how much I love our community and how grateful I am to be part of it. I feel acknowledged and appreciated by the community that surrounds my school. The experience invigorates me, inspires me, and makes me want to stay forever.

● ● ●

I've often heard principals lament the loneliness they feel in their job. I don't believe it has to be that way. Loneliness sprouts and festers when we don't feel connected to others around us, but connectedness is a choice, no? It takes an investment of time and energy, a willingness to evolve in our communication practices, and an approach characterized by creativity and out-of-the-box thinking—but the payoff will be rich and meaningful for everyone involved.

Reinvest: Expanding Relationships with Staff and Students

Every Monday morning, principals and teachers walk into school, preprogrammed for the same start:

> "Good morning," we greet one another. "How was your weekend?"
>
> "Fine. Yours?"
>
> "Fine. Thanks."

And thus begins another week of similar, predictable conversations and interactions. We check in with staff, often through bland and rote interactions. To our internal shame, we sometimes avoid people with whom we have tense or awkward relationships, ducking into doorways or taking a different hallway. It's easier that way, right?

In this chapter, we will jump out of those constraints, break routines, and offer inspiration to work toward more meaningful relationships with those around us—namely, our students and our staff. Let's begin by reexamining our connection and rapport with our staff.

Connecting with Staff

The adults who work in schools are a complicated mix of personalities, and they hold a variety of philosophies. We have our eternal optimists—teachers who bounce in every morning and greet the day with positivity and a willingness to take on any challenge. Conversely, every staff has those teachers who feel like dead weight—negative, cynical, and toxic to the positive mission of the school. And, of course, there's everyone in between.

It is easy for principals to get distracted and disenchanted in efforts to navigate around and through the needs of all their staff members. I tend to rely too much on my Pollyannas, counting on them to lift the demeanor of others, while I waste precious energy trying to manage my Negative Nellies. It is a never-ending dance, with the potential to leave me grumpy and dismissive—traits that are not good for a principal's career longevity, job satisfaction, or leadership prowess.

How, then, can we double down on our efforts to engage staff members on their own merits and territory without adding more to our workday or zapping our energy? Can we reinforce the positive behaviors of role-model teachers at the same time we improve the efforts and spirits of the ones dragging us down? In this section, we will discuss ways to actively reacquaint ourselves with staff, particularly in terms of the successes and challenges facing teachers in their personal and professional lives.

Connect Personally

As principals, we are all much more than our professional role (an idea we will revisit again in Chapter 8), and this is true, too, of teachers and other staff members. They are much more than the glimpse we might see in a brief visit to a classroom. Because teaching is the kind of job in which feedback comes largely from students and parents, teachers generally crave a genuine connection with their principal and deeply appreciate acknowledgment of their "whole self."

Given the routines and predictability of a school year, this notion can too easily be forgotten, so we frequently let our relationships with teachers grow stale and routine. Let's ask a few self-reflective questions to rekindle efforts toward having a tight, powerful force uniting the principal and teachers.

Do I know my staff members individually? *All* **of them?** One of the teachers in my building was a quiet, private soul. She did nice work in the classroom; her students enjoyed her class; data showed they were achieving in line with peers across the school and district. I had a positive relationship with her, though it was, admittedly, a surface-only professional connection. I rarely needed to intervene or defend her. She worked independently and usually left school right at our release time. Everything was . . . *fine.* For several years, we coexisted without a blip.

Imagine my surprise, then, when someone mentioned in passing, "Did you see Mrs. O's latest webpage?" I had no idea what she was talking about.

"You didn't know? As a side hobby, she highlights various places around the state where parents can take their children for a fun, educational day out."

What?

"And you should see her photography!"

A few clicks online, and there it was: sweet, quiet Mrs. O maintained a website with stunning photographs accompanied by delightful, funny anecdotes of weekend adventures, highlighting well-hidden "secret" destinations within a day's drive of our city. She had an admirable eye with a camera; her photographs positively gleamed with beautiful tricks of light. She was, in ways I'd never known, a deeply talented artist.

I went to ask her about it—several times. I was fascinated by her complicated, twisty story about her professional journey, her decision to devote time to a personal website, and how she applied her talents to her work in the classroom. She wasn't seeking fame or fortune with her writing or photography; she only wanted enjoyment and fulfillment, which she found with her small but passionate group of loyal followers.

How had I not known this? How had I gone several years working with this woman but never probed into the person she was outside school? *Shameful,* I chastised myself, and I promised to do better.

Am I giving too much time and energy to certain people at the expense of others? We all have staff members who take up vast amounts of our time and energy. They need frequent affirmations, regular check-ins, and a consistent visibility. We oblige, making ourselves omnipresent for those staff members. The problem? Our behavior can quickly become a habit, and we stop seeing the needs of our lower-maintenance staff members, who are soldiering on in the background. We assume they are doing just fine, and we even begin taking them for granted. We might, then, miss an opportunity for a rich relationship or overlook talent we could use to help our school. After realizing the depth of Mrs. O's creative flair, for example, I asked her to lend her calligraphy-like penmanship to the front cover of a student-led school poetry book. She was thrilled to help out, and her artistic essence enhanced a project created for our entire school.

Is the negativity of others wearing me down? Being a principal can feel like being a tree trunk with thousands of woodpeckers constantly peck, peck, pecking. Especially on long days or during difficult times of the year, we can become victims of staff members who suck the energy from our souls. We all have those teachers and staff members who are negative and pernicious. They question everything we do, often in whispers behind our backs. They are never happy. Yet we try—oh, how we continue to try.

Dealing with toxic staff members feels like any unhealthy relationship. It can be an all-consuming cycle of hurt and stress that we somehow believe is our fault. We hold out hope that if we just find the magic formula, "Next time will certainly be better" or "*I* am the one who can change this person." So we keep going back and trying again. But at what cost? A high one, unfortunately, because what we stand to lose is our spirit, our positivity, and our zest for leadership.

Decades of teachers' lounge observations have taught us this truth: when we surround ourselves with others who choose positivity, we stay positive, upbeat, and forward moving; when we are buried in negative attitudes and toxicity, we cannot hold back the tide of negativity ourselves. It becomes who we become.

I think of the graphic in Figure 3.1 when deciding how to allocate my time—not the *quantity* of time, because all teachers should have a relatively equal allocation, but what I *do* with my time. Teachers in either of the lower blocks (weak teacher/positive attitude and weak teacher/toxic, negative attitude) need my focus to get them to an upper block. Teachers in the upper-right block (strong teacher/toxic, negative attitude) need me to try to shift them to the upper-left block (strong teacher/positive attitude). Any teacher in the right column is going to require delicate and careful work on my part, but I'd much rather have a teacher anywhere in the left column than wallowing on the right.

FIGURE 3.1
Teachers and Attitudes: Four Combinations

Strong teacher Positive attitude	Strong teacher Toxic, negative attitude
Weak teacher Positive attitude	Weak teacher Toxic, negative attitude

A side note: I actually learn a lot from negative, toxic teachers. They remind me of the educator I never want to become and prompt me to check my negativity barometer frequently. Am I growing disenchanted? Am I complaining about things outside my circle of influence? Am I blaming others for things that make me uncomfortable or unhappy? If I answer a couple of those questions with a yes, it's time to pull away from negativity and find my way back to leading a staff made up of strong teachers with a positive, uplifting attitude.

How can principals think differently about connecting with staff members? We all have our standard check-in opportunities: quick chats before meetings, casual conversations at the copy machine, stop-in visits before and after school. But these expeditious visits can't provide the depth we need to truly connect. Further, the standard staff social setting—an after-school "happy hour"—can be uncomfortable for principals: *Should I go? Should I not? How long should I stay? Will I stifle the staff camaraderie if I go?* As a simple solution, many of us choose to avoid them. So what's a principal to do? Let's take a look at a few ideas.

Use social media. If you want to watch a spirited debate, ask a group of principals their thoughts on whether they should be Facebook friends with staff or interact with them on Instagram. There is no one correct answer, because each of us has our own thoughts about social media. Some principals eschew the very idea; they want more limits and control over their private lives and personal time. I completely understand and support that stance. With that said, I do accept staff members as Facebook friends, and I quite enjoy the opportunity. I see it as a practical and convenient tool to connect with my staff. I do stick to a few simple parameters: I don't request "friends" but happily accept them; I only comment on a post if it is positive or supportive; and I never post anything on my page beyond a few profile pictures or holiday greetings. Having a social media connection with staff provides a permission-based peek into their lives, interests, and experiences, which launches great conversations I would never have without the prompt taken from social media. This goes for Twitter and Instagram, too.

Of course, if you choose not to connect using social media, that's OK too. There are many other unplugged ways to do it, including the following suggestions.

Host coffees or office hours. Many superintendents offer dates and times when the public can come sit and talk in a restaurant or coffee shop. Principals, particularly of large schools, might consider doing the same for their staff members—right at school. I know of a principal of a large urban school who sets aside two mornings a week when he promises he'll be in his office. He picks up a couple dozen donuts, brews a pot of coffee, and welcomes staff members to stop by for conversation. Although visits frequently begin with a school-related question, he tries to make an authentic connection with colleagues through his self-challenge to get to know them on a personal level.

Encourage wellness. How might your staff get better together? Because we generally spend more of our waking hours with the people we work with than with anyone else in our lives, our workmates can become accountability partners in all things related to wellness. You can call a gym or fitness studio and ask for a reduced rate for a group class for your staff, host a cooking class at school using lounge or kitchen space, or throw out wellness challenges with incentives and prizes. Beyond the obvious health benefits, these types of activities tend to create or reestablish relationships with staff on a personal level.

A friend of mine launched a weekly after-school walking club for teachers. It was an unstructured open invitation to walk around campus grounds and the school's neighborhood and, in inclement weather, in the school hallways. Walking is, of course, an excellent way to eliminate stress and increase health and wellness. It is also a fantastic way to connect with someone else, because stride-for-stride conversation feels safe and encourages an openness that doesn't happen in traditional professional settings. My friend cranks up the music on the P.A. and joins teachers as they walk. He learns a lot about his staff in ways he couldn't using traditional attempts at communication.

Engage in games or challenges. The possibilities are endless here. Trivia contests, sports-bracketing polls, school bingo games in the lounge with positive connection–building challenges and prizes, flashback quizzes—anything fun that will evoke giggles and conversation is a way to enhance your connection with your staff. I once took a precious hour from an all-school professional development day to do a "Two Truths and a Lie" activity with my staff. We laughed, we shared stories, and we enjoyed time together in a brand-new way. I truly believe that "lost" hour gained us more than we'd gotten from full days of unconnected meetings.

Share a personal learning experience. In recent years, I've provided staff with copies of some provocative and timely texts, on a completely voluntary basis, and facilitated casual talks about these books before school. We've read Michele Borba's *Unselfie,* Kate Fagan's *What Made Maddy Run,* Hans Rosling's *Factfulness,* and Gavin de Becker's *Protecting the Gift: Keeping Children and Teenagers Safe (and Parents Sane).* Although these books could be considered professional reads, they are also deeply personal; we can all relate to the topics they cover, both in our own lives and experiences and in the lives of others around us. Because many of our staff members are parents grappling with their own struggles raising children in a complicated, social media–driven world, our book conversations take on a rich, individualized tone. Staff members are grateful for the chance to talk in a safe environment full of empathetic listeners.

This idea could be replicated for any format, by the way. Podcasts, movies, and documentaries can all spark thought-provoking conversations among colleagues.

Listen. Too many times I get caught up in the hustle of a school day and don't read signs telling me to slow down and really listen when a staff member needs to talk. I was reminded of this not long ago when a teacher stopped in "just to say hi." She leaned against the door jamb in my office, hesitating somewhat. It occurred to me, vaguely at first, "She seems to want to talk." I invited her to have a seat while I readjusted myself into a listening mindset. She told me about some upcoming appointments that would require her to leave just a few minutes before her contractual time. "No problem," I said. "Is everything OK?" Not really, she said. She'd recently been diagnosed with generalized anxiety disorder. She was hesitant to tell me, she said, because she didn't want me to think there was anything "different" or "wrong" with her. Indeed, she was scared to tell anyone. But she was relieved too, because she finally had a diagnosis and an explanation for a lifetime of struggles. I listened carefully and respectfully, waiting until she was all talked out before offering an acknowledgment of her feelings and affirmation of my continued love and respect for her.

Make room for mental health challenges. As in the experience just described, I am constantly reminded how, as a society, we are hesitant to share, acknowledge, and accept mental health struggles in others and ourselves. We all have issues, to some extent, yet we all fear revealing too much to colleagues. I aspire to be a principal who stands firmly balanced between honoring privacy and being a safe place for any staff member who needs help or support. There are times I don't need to be The Boss; instead, I can be a friend, resource, and buttress of strength. Brave teachers will tell their truth—but only if they trust their principal not to judge, dismiss, or discriminate.

Have fun in a unique way. Many staffs have regular happy hours, but why not funnel the benefits of staff social time into something fun, productive, and all-inclusive? Here are some ideas:

- *Produce a faculty show or skit.* Rehearsals are a hoot, and students will be delighted!
- *Attend a play or performance together.* A couple winters ago, many members of our staff came together and attended a professional stage production of *Wicked*. We dressed up, had a delicious dinner out, and shared an arts performance. We had a lovely time unplugging from our typical environment and found ourselves talking about the experience for months.
- *Tour local facilities, universities, or organizations.* Possible destinations are sports arenas, museums, production factories, flourishing businesses, or even a nearby "natural wonder." Beyond the secondary benefit of experiences we can share with students that could assist with college and career choices, these tours can be a unique shared experience for staff members.
- *Create an* Amazing Race *experience* with stops around the community.
- *Host a summer retreat* with absolutely no "official business"— just fun. I have colleagues who have done this with canoeing, bowling, cookouts, games, scavenger hunts, and all sorts

of other relationship-building entertainment. Invite staff members to bring kids and families, and you've got unlimited opportunities to connect with staff members.

Ask, "What brought you here?" A friend of mine had an epiphany one day when he realized that he knew where only a handful of his staff of 80 had gone to high school, college, or graduate school. Most of them had been hired before he'd been named the building principal, so he never saw their résumés; for teachers he *had* hired, he'd forgotten that particular detail in the hustle and bustle of the hiring process. He made it his mission to find out. He filled a jar with slips of paper, each with a staff member's name on it, and pulled out two or three every day. Then he'd track down those staff members and launch a conversation: *Where did you grow up? Where did you go to school? How much education did you get? What starts, stops, and twists came along the way? What degrees do you hold? What certifications do you have?*

He had a ball. He was thrilled to learn so much about the personal and professional journeys of his staff. He was dismayed, too, to recognize just how little he'd known about them. One of his quietest, sweetest paraprofessionals had been a highly skilled corporate insurance investigator and then was a stay-at-home parent for a decade before rejoining the workforce in a lower-stress school environment. Another teacher had been a four-year All-American swimmer on the team of a prominent university. Yet another was a classically trained opera singer. So inspired was he by the connections he made with his staff, connections frequently based on where and when they'd been educated, that he decided to buy nameplates for each staff member with whatever school logo they wanted to honor. When the nameplates arrived and were posted outside each classroom, the whole staff was buzzing with questions and stories they shared with one another. Then the students started in. Teachers were talking with students about their educational journeys, the twists and turns their lives had taken, and how they came to teach there, at that school, at that point in time. It was like an ongoing "career day" experience for students and staff alike. Powerful, no?

Connect Professionally

As the example about school nameplates illustrates, it's all too easy to know terribly little about our staff members on a personal level. Even more surprising may be the mysteries they hold professionally. You see teachers and staff members immersed in their roles every day at work, but annual evaluations aside, what might you not know about your staff as professionals? Are there ways you can boost your own professional energy by sharing a professional journey with teachers in your building? Here are a few ideas to provoke thought and move toward mutually beneficial professional connections.

Attend conferences as a team or staff. Attending conferences as a team can create a professional bond with staff members in unexpected ways. Too few principals put value on this experience, held back by the expense or logistics of planning a professional trip. But traveling together is always a bonding experience, delays and challenges notwithstanding; so, too, is the experience of poring over a conference brochure, divvying up the sessions to attend, and talking over dinner about what has been learned and how it might be implemented at school. After-hours are fun, too; people feel more comfortable letting their hair down when home responsibilities disappear. We talk a lot about knowing the "whole child" at school, but knowing the "whole adult" is just as helpful.

Present together. You know how refreshing it is to get together with other people who share your interests and passions? The same kind of enjoyment can happen when staff members examine professional practices together by developing a presentation to share with colleagues. Whether locally (a professional development event hosted at or by your school building) or at state or national conferences, sharing professional knowledge is a bonding exercise. It will stretch you to discover new things: which strategies colleagues use in presenting to other educators, ideas for adding a digital component to a presentation, which handouts and supports to offer your attendees, how to capture audience feedback and respond to their questions. The experience will help you and your team build confidence, knowledge, skills, and passion—together.

Take on a tough task alongside teachers. Professional conversations with teachers typically happen during the evaluation process, which can be anxiety provoking and difficult for everyone. In a lot of ways, I dislike how prohibitive evaluations can be because of implications of punitive or correctional action. If we remove that aspect and replace it with situations where we are connecting casually and in a healthy, favorable environment, we can make fantastic connections with teachers.

Recently, I spent a great deal of time in a special education classroom. We had enrolled an extremely intense student who was prone to furious outbursts and self-injury. I spent a lot of time sitting on the floor with the teacher as we supported the student through his anger, tears, and then the silent period he needed to recompose himself. I was there for two reasons: first, policy required two trained staff members to be present when a student was in crisis, and I was trained *and* had the flexible time needed; second, I *wanted* to be there with the teacher. We talked for hours over the course of the year, growing quite close as comrades and colleagues. It's not always possible to build such a tight professional connection, but a great starting point is jumping in the trenches with teachers and taking advantage of the learning that can be found there.

Join in instructional coaching. If your school is lucky enough to have instructional coaches for teachers and if your district protocols allow it, a rich learning experience can result from joining in the debriefing conversations a teacher might have with a coach. This situation isn't always possible or even wise; respecting confidentiality is a big component in successful teacher-coach relationships. But if the conditions are right, a teacher might love to have you listen in during a conversation about the craft of teaching. Recently, a teacher invited me to join one of her informal walk-throughs as she debriefed with the coach. It was a special and unconventional way for me to really see how the teacher was thinking about her students and their learning.

Conduct no-agenda classroom visits. Teachers astound me with their patience and focus on students. I love casual visits to classrooms where I just stop in, ask teachers if they need anything, and throw out an on-point compliment (e.g., "Look how engaged that group of students is!" or "It seems that our new student has acclimated beautifully in your class" or "That's one of my favorite texts; I'm so glad you're using it in your classroom"). I find such enjoyment in seeing teachers working their magic with patience and concentration, and when I take the time to tell them how much I admire their work, it creates an attachment beyond our standard systems and practices.

Respond to book wish lists. If you have the budget to do it, invite each teacher to choose a book and then purchase it for them. No limits, no constraints; just the gift of a book—or two. When the books arrive, hand-deliver them all and, if teachers offer the information, take some time to discover why they chose that particular book.

Identify Long-Term Goals

Principals routinely work with staff to set short-term goals for the year, often during pre-evaluation meetings when we review assessment data. We talk about goals, and we set appropriate progress-monitoring protocols. It's quite rare, though, that we work with our staff to consider a plan for an entire career.

When I'd just started as a teacher, my principal mentioned that I might want to someday be a principal. I scoffed at the suggestion, but the tiny seed had been planted. It lay dormant for a while, even as I grew restless as a teacher. It didn't begin to bloom until a conversation with my next principal. She sat down with me and launched a deep, heartfelt conversation about—well, about the rest of my life. If not for her genuine interest in my long-term professional goals, I don't know what path my career may have taken. I enjoy paying her gift forward, intentionally doing the same with my own staff members. It's selfish, too, in a way, because I find great personal invigoration in helping them think through what they want to do years down the road. I like feeling I might be making a true difference for others by asking mentoring questions: *What kind of professional do you want to be? What steps might you take now to make sure it happens? Should you seek additional endorsements and certifications? Might you need experience with extracurricular activities or supplemental roles to help build your résumé?*

Scatter Seeds for Growth and Change

I try to keep up an ongoing conversation with staff members so I always know how they feel about their current teaching positions. When I know someone is restless or eager for a new challenge, I file the information and keep my eye out for openings and positions that might be a perfect fit—thereby making sure everyone is in the right places, doing the things they want to do. Thus, when I need to make some staff changes within our school, I rarely have to move someone to a different role or grade level against his or her wishes.

Not long ago, I worked with a teacher who had taught the same thing for many years. She was very good at her job and saw no need to change anything; she had the curriculum and sequence of her year on autopilot. But I had my suspicions that she was bored. In casual conversation one day, I asked her if she'd ever considered a different grade level. No way, she said.

"Why?" I asked.

"I . . . well, I guess . . . I guess I don't really know," she admitted.

She couldn't give me a single reason not to think of something else. So I told her about an unexpected opening in a different grade level for the coming year. I gave her a list of reasons why I wanted her to consider taking the spot. I saw her make a shift in her mind as I deliberately built her confidence and excitement.

"I'll think about it," she said.

A few days passed, and she told me she was considering the change. After a few more days, she said it might be something she'd like to do. And after few *more* days, she was all in—even begging me to make the change official so the chance wouldn't get away. When given time, most teachers—not all—really enjoy a new challenge. They find it validating and complimentary to be asked to apply their talents in a new role.

In another example, a special education teacher had devoted his career to helping students with academic, social, and emotional needs. I asked him if he'd ever considered school counseling. He looked at me like I had said something preposterous—but just for a moment. "I'd never thought of that for myself," he said slowly. He marinated in the idea for a while and then told me, "You might be right. I suspect I would love being a guidance counselor." Not long afterward, he took the plunge: he went back to graduate school to secure his counseling degree and plans to finish his career as a high school guidance counselor. He thanks me often for recognizing the talent and experience required to land him in a new position doing (his words) "exactly what I'm supposed to be doing right now." His energy boost has become my energy boost, partly because I'm so genuinely happy that he is happy, and partly because I see a renewed enthusiasm in him that transfers directly to students and their success.

Connecting with Students

Principals can always reinvest in relationships with students, particularly by modeling an enhanced commitment to know (and correctly pronounce!) student names and really understand individual stories. Even better, and more far-reaching, is empowering teachers and support staff to do the same. The effort goes beyond "Student of the Month" celebrations or honoring high-achieving students for their accomplishments; it also goes beyond the natural and traditional "lift up" of the athletes, musicians, and artists in our schools.

This section will help you consider ways school staff can truly get to know students' personal stories and highlight the hopes, dreams, and goals of each student on a schoolwide scale. In some cases, doing so first requires working through challenges in our relationships with students, including overcoming bias, resisting premature conclusions, and addressing mental health issues. Such efforts create a sturdier platform for constructing positive and productive staff-student relationships.

Catch Bias

In her powerful book *Culturally Responsive Teaching and the Brain,* Zaretta Hammond (2015) discusses the negative effect of microaggressions, those "small seemingly innocuous brief verbal, behavioral, or environmental indignities that send hostile, derogatory, denigrating, and hurtful messages to people of color" (p. 112). Indeed, hostile or derogatory language or actions can contribute to negativity bias for any student—that is, a student's brain will remember and respond "to negative experiences up to three times more than positive experiences" (p. 113). Isn't that shocking? Frightening? Isn't it worth our while to do anything we can to avoid microaggressive behavior? Hammond also addresses microassaults, microinsults, and microinvalidations, highlighting the impact of the interactions we have with students and how important it is that educators check their bias at the door.

Adults (and students) must constantly resist the tendency to make sweeping judgments or assumptions about others based on standing societal beliefs. I have this tendency myself. We all do. Knowing the impact they can have, though, I look for them, actively, so I can think about them, talk about them, bring them into the light, quiet them, and eliminate them. And such judgments and assumptions are everywhere. It is impossible to list them all, and certainly impossible to even mention the most obvious ones without offending, but some common examples are assumptions we make about a family unit. If a child is being raised by a single parent, we may fail to consider certain possibilities—an amicable divorce, for example, with the absent parent living far away—and instead jump to the conclusion that the absent parent is a deadbeat or is in some sort of trouble (drugs? alcohol? jail?). Single parents, we assume, have made bad decisions or are the victims of someone else's bad decisions. In another example, we may assume that children in foster care are miserable, lonely, doomed. Racial and gender assumptions run rampant too: African American students will be athletes; Asian students will be math- and science-focused, driven by zealous parents; Latino students will be transient; girls will be girls and boys will be boys.

As the examples in Figure 3.2 (p. 65) illustrate, aside from biased judgments along gender or racial and ethnic lines, misassumptions can be about simple things, too. My sister's friend experienced this not long ago. Her son's school counselor called to report that he was "unclean." Taken aback, she asked for more details. "I don't know specifics," the counselor admitted in a tone of distaste. "Some students at his table have reported an unpleasant odor." She went on to express concern about his "dirty clothing" and "unkempt appearance." The tone and implications were deeply hurtful. I know this boy. He is an impish, garrulous ball of energy who has, since he could walk, taken a "parkour" approach to making his way through the world—running, climbing, leaping, and vaulting from place to place. Did he arrive at school with dirt on his shirt? Certainly he did. Was he neglected, impoverished, unclean, living in squalor? Not in the least. But that's not even the point. What if the suspicions had been spot-on? What if there had been issues at home contributing to the boy's rumpled, unkempt appearance? Would a condescending phone call to the parent, delivered in a critical and judgmental tone, have benefited anyone? What a shame, how often students (and their parents) have to disprove the assumptions made against them—often unknowingly, always unfairly.

Ironically, education gives us the platform to change assumptions and bias, but frequently (usually unconsciously) we actually deepen them because of our own aspirations to educational sainthood. Most of us went into this profession because we want to make a difference in a big way. We saw the movies *Dangerous Minds* and *Stand and Deliver,* and we heard inspirational stories of teachers who swooped in to change a child's wayward life trajectory. We, too, were inspired to make a life's work out of transforming young lives, of really *seeing* a child, of identifying that child's *real* needs before anyone else does. We lie in wait till we can jump in and be someone's hero. All admirable. The problem? Too often we jump too quickly. We don't pause to examine our latent bias in learning a student's story. We end up committing all kinds of unforgivable microaggressions—against the very people we are trying to help.

It is up to us, as principals, to muster the courage to lead this conversation, uncomfortable as it is, in the context of getting to know our students. We need to ask hard questions when we see microaggressions and insensitivities. Addressing them doesn't require accusations; again, teachers have only the best of intentions. Instead, we

FIGURE 3.2

Check Your Assumptions

A student who is . . .	Is not necessarily . . .
Quiet	Shy, anxious, or nervous
Rumpled or unkempt	Living in poverty or neglect
Living with one parent	Sad, lonely, or "missing" something
Wearing the same clothing repeatedly	Poor or exhibiting sensory or compulsive behaviors
Exhibiting a particular odor	Uneducated about proper hygiene
Exhibiting early sexual or romantic attraction toward others	A victim of abuse
Indifferent about school	Avoiding schoolwork or missing a connection with the "right teacher"
Male	Athletic, energetic, loud, or aggressive
Female	Sensitive, dramatic, compliant, or eager to please
A minority	Lacking a sense of belonging
An English learner	Confused, unhappy, or "lost"

can nudge our staff to consider their own bias by kindly, gently, and thoughtfully asking questions such as these:

- What assumptions are we making about students?
- Are our latent biases influencing our decisions when we work with students?
- If we feel or see bias, what do we do about it?
- If a student is displaying negative behaviors, low self-confidence, lack of efficacy, or a general malaise about school, what negative experiences may have contributed to the situation? What can be done to reverse the tide?
- As a whole, how are we doing in overcoming bias and its negative impact on our students?

Using these questions when working with staff may provoke deep thinking and enhance professional growth. During this process, keep in mind that there is a lot about us that no one knows. Our stories are complex and deep, with many branches of pain, perseverance, and purpose. As a collective whole, we should avoid making assumptions about others or accusing them of bias without seeking to understand them or communicate in a real or purposeful way. Principals can model this reinvestment in student relationships by broaching difficult topics and conversations with staff about how we talk to kids, the relationships we build with them, and our role in their lives.

Slow the Train Before It Derails

Getting to know students takes time. I am frequently reminded of this. Recently, a new student came to our school and immediately displayed concerning behaviors. She was disruptive and combative and refused to comply with basic classroom expectations. Her first day sent the teacher into a tailspin. As the buses pulled out after dismissal, I found him pacing outside my office. He outlined the student's offenses, detailing each transgression, and insisted we immediately reallocate support staff so an aide could be with her throughout the day. He ended by saying, "On top of her behaviors, she is also *very* far behind in her reading and writing. She will need intervention support."

"OK," I said, seeking to counter his anxiety with calm and reason. "Let's start with her name." I picked up my pencil. "Last name first."

"Z—," he said.

I waited.

"It starts with a *Z*. It's . . . uh . . . well . . . ."

I stared at him. Here he was, having profiled her as behaviorally and academically in crisis, and he didn't yet know her full name.

"Tell you what," I said. "Let's first get to know this child's story. I'm not saying it will make our path any different; I'm just saying we should know her before we make any big decisions."

Later he revealed I'd made him feel chastised, but he grudgingly admitted I'd been right. To his credit, he went right to work, inviting her to have lunch with him to talk about her past school experiences and asking her father to come in for a get-to-know-you meeting. He read files from her previous school and supplemented the data with some formative assessment of his own. He met with the guidance counselor and Response to Intervention coach. Her behaviors did not disappear; in fact, eventually interventions were indeed put in place to address some deeper issues. But we learned much more about her, including her strength in academics. By getting to know her, the teacher was able to speak more intelligently and thoughtfully about her needs. He has since become a pied piper of sorts with his colleagues, repeating this story and urging them to slow down and get to know students before deciding who they are.

Focus on Mental Health

It's no secret that our students are facing a withering sense of self-efficacy, along with anxiety and stress at levels we are unused to. According to the Pew Research Center (Horowitz & Graf, 2019), 7 in 10 teens see anxiety and depression as concerns among their peers. We can begin to address this situation by seeking to understand what struggles students are facing and being aware of the issues that trip them up. To that end, let's remember how much power comes with knowledge.

I am fortunate to work in a district that has reallocated resources to increase our focus on student mental health. We've partnered with community counseling services, increased student support services staff, and provided specific training for staff on anxiety, overuse of social media, suicide prevention, and crisis management. Of course, the increased efforts don't feel like victory; we desperately wish we didn't need such training and support systems. But as a principal, I'm so glad we invest in this way. I feel prepared and empowered to handle the sad inevitability of student crisis. After all, as we all know, navigating issues with student mental health is tricky for principals. On the one hand, we carry the heavy weight of responsibility for the manifestations of student issues, whether it is the impact on that student's selfhood or on the rest of the student body. On the other hand, we can't tackle the issue alone; we need our entire teaching and support staff to have their eyes, ears, and hearts open to the students who need help. Investing in mental health addresses both these problems.

Avoid Judgment and Assumptions

I am convinced judgment is the hidden ingredient in toxic relationships, whether they are with adults or students—maybe especially with students, who sometimes make poor decisions for all sorts of reasons, including legitimate ones, if seen from their perspective. And when they make a decision that lands them in trouble or crisis, what makes it worse is judgment from the principal or teacher. Kids *hate* to be judged. They can sense it and are repelled by it, especially if we trip over ourselves saying, "I'm not judging!" That's how they know we already have.

Approaching students with a clean, factual lens is much more helpful than going in with minds made up. Avoiding assumptions is similar to avoiding judgment. It's difficult to do, but essential if we want to have a genuine connection with students.

Many years ago, in my first job as an administrator, we had a student—we'll call her Saria—who had some physical challenges and had an appearance resembling that of children with fetal alcohol syndrome. She was a sweet, passive student most of the time, though prone to occasional outbursts of frustration and sadness. Her Individualized Education Program (IEP) addressed speech and language, occupational therapy, and adapted physical education.

I made assumptions about this child I am embarrassed to admit on paper. Based solely on her appearance and intervention support, I assumed she had significantly limited cognitive ability.

As part of our regular evaluation process, our school administered a broad school-ability assessment, and I was dumbfounded when I flipped through the results. Saria had the highest school-ability index in the entire school. I flipped through more data. She was one of only three students in the entire district who'd capped out on the assessment. The child's full-scale IQ was the highest I'd ever seen.

The test score shifted my view of this child, but here's the truth: *it shouldn't have had to.* I should have known better. I should have overcome the instant conclusions that are drawn when we first meet someone and assume we know that person's story. It was a hard and humbling lesson, and one I think of often, partly because I'm so embarrassed and ashamed of myself, but also because it's a human tendency to judge and conclude, and I need to make a conscious effort to transcend that tendency. I'm not always successful, but oh, do I try.

Learn Students' Histories

Some teachers feel strongly that they should give students a "fresh start" at the beginning of the school year. Noble and fervent in their stance, they refuse to look backward—which includes studying a student's cumulative files or collecting data about previous years' performances, struggles, or interventions. What a shame, I think; negligent, too. I tell teachers their professional duty is to learn the story of students so they know how best to help them. That advice doesn't negate a fresh start. We can do both: get to know each child's story and then leave our bias behind.

Support and Empower Teachers' Efforts

Setting expectations about how to connect with students is an excellent way to expand teacher capacity. After all, teachers are the ones standing alongside students during the educational process. They are the ones who can, will, and should get to know their students, in real time and in real ways. As a principal, I can make a bigger and more significant impact if I empower teachers to deepen their own relationship-building efforts and rely on them to be the main point of contact and connection with students.

I once led a workshop with staff from another school in which I asked teachers to outline what they'd like people to know about them. I used a "know this, not that" format as a launch. After a powerful hour of writing, thinking, and sharing, we planned how to replicate the writing activity for students. It offered a specific structure they could use to get to know the students *as the students wanted to be known*. I followed up with the principal some months later, and he shared some of the writing from students in an English class:

KNOW THIS: I want to be a good writer. NOT THAT: I used to get in a lot of trouble in school. A LOT.

KNOW THIS: I have five siblings. NOT THAT: I am the only one of my family who hates sports.

KNOW THIS: I love Fortnite. NOT THAT: I am terrible in math.

KNOW THIS: I want to go to college and make new friends. NOT THAT: I have no clue what my major should be!

If we really think about these snippets, we see that they reveal much beyond the facts stated on the paper. The "know this" component reveals the student's current realities, laced with a good dose of their hopes and dreams; the "not that" portion reveals their fears, embarrassments, or history. Both can serve as substantial launchpads for authentic connections with students.

Principals can provide both the structure and the freedom for teachers to get to know their students with some sort of exercise that models ways to get at who we are, who we used to be, and who we want to be. It's an investment that will pay off immeasurably.

● ● ●

I used to set a goal to get to know the name and story of every student in my building. I truly thought I could do it, but I've since learned I really can't. There are just too many of them and not enough of me. So there are always students I know well, students I sort of know, and students I know hardly at all. There are many more on the "know hardly at all" end of the spectrum than on the "know well" end.

So what do I do? One thing: *keep trying*. That's where I find my peace—in my unrelenting effort to be every student's best principal. I believe that we all find the right person to connect with when we need to connect. I don't want to force myself on any student who doesn't need or want my input, but I want to be a positive life-changer for a student who does. In some way, I want to touch everyone, even if the connection is several degrees removed. I strive to be part of a broad, powerful circle of educators, standing together in active outreach, with students at the center. I count that as the best I can do.

Revamp Instructional Leadership: Shaping Instruction for Today's World

Sometimes leading instruction feels like catching fish with bare hands: it sounds doable and should get easier with experience and patience, but it's *always* slippery and unpredictable. Being an instructional leader takes instinct, a continual commitment to learn, and ongoing perseverance. But when it works, isn't it fun? Exciting? Immensely rewarding?

The foundations of good instruction stay largely the same over time, but the tools we use when teaching can—and absolutely should—change and evolve. As principals, we are charged with being the instructional leaders of a school, and we can find great energy and excitement by leading teachers out of outdated, mundane learning experiences and toward innovative instructional practices.

In this chapter, we'll consider how we can thoughtfully and deliberately guide teachers to take risks and how to celebrate the rewards of doing so. Specifically, we'll find ways to avoid "packet teaching" that relies on worksheets or busywork; reconsider homework policies; cast a critical eye on vendor-based programs; embrace new ways of providing high-quality instruction, including project-based learning and blended learning opportunities; and incorporate innovation and creativity into classroom routines.

Let's start by reviewing what we know about good instruction. We know to look for these things when visiting classrooms and evaluating teachers:

- Teachers making a connection to their students by getting to know them as individuals and learners
- Teachers searching for areas of interest and strength in students
- Consistent use of differentiation and personalization in instructional delivery so each student is an engaged and productive learner

With that foundation, we can inspire our schools' teachers and classrooms—and ourselves—by revamping how instruction should look, especially now that we are well into the 21st century. We can start by abandoning practices that are no longer applicable or appropriate, and bravely supporting teachers who try innovative and inspiring ways to teach.

Abandoning the Old

So many times we equate "taking a risk" with daring to try something new. In a classroom, however, taking a risk might mean having the courage to let go of traditional practices that no longer have value beyond habit or nostalgia and that may, in fact, inhibit progress or innovation. Many teachers hesitate to abandon what feels "safe" and "acceptable" without securing the principal's blessing, which we can't offer unless we do some deep thinking. Here, we'll look at three traditional teaching practices that it might be time to abandon, adjust, or reassess: packets, homework, and vendor-based programs.

Eliminate Packets

Nothing makes me cringe like a "packet teacher." I *hate* packets. They are a façade masquerading as good teaching. They *appear* to keep students engaged and productive, and they produce a "product" that is easy to grade summatively. That's why the use of packets can look and feel like good teaching.

It's not.

Although I squirm to admit it, I was a packet teacher long ago. I'd been given a lot of packets as a student, so I assumed that's what I should do. I followed a standard, predictable packet schedule. Every Sunday night I'd go into school and make sets of grammar worksheets, neatly stapled together. On Monday mornings I would hand them to my students with the assignment (an admonition, really) to complete them by the end of the week. "Read the directions at the top of each page and complete each worksheet in the packet," I'd say. *That* was my instruction. Then I'd add, "Make sure you put your name on the packet. If you don't, you'll automatically lose five points." I'd collect the packets on Friday—from those who had completed them—and spend all weekend grading them, plugging the scores into my grade book. The whole thing reset again on Sunday. During the week, we worked on other things in class, but I reminded the students about The Packet every day. "Don't forget. Due on Friday," I'd say. Often.

I apologize—to all the students I had in that first year, and their parents. The experience must have been miserable. It took some pointed questions from a forward-thinking curriculum leader to stop my packet passion and challenge me to think differently, to put in the effort and time required to break away from packets forever. Ironically, abandoning packets actually freed up immense amounts of time; rather than grading hundreds of fill-in-the-blank worksheets or trying to decipher whether my students had put commas in the right place, I evolved to spending my weekends thinking about my students as writers, reading new books so I could make good recommendations, and creating interesting prompts to launch a writing project they'd love.

Packets are relics in today's classroom, and principals can help teachers abandon them by sharing these basic truths:

- Packet completion rewards compliance and diligence.
  Students who need a personalized touch or teacher-inspired

motivation will falter beneath the weight of packet-based teaching.

- Packets foster exactly zero thought beyond rote memorization or plugging information into blank spots on a worksheet.
- Packets stifle creativity.
- Packets offer no opportunity for collaboration (unless it is copying from a classmate).
- Managing packets takes valuable time away from real teaching and learning.
- Packet completion does not lead to deep understanding or applicability of knowledge.
- There is no real way to know who, exactly, is completing packets. A diligent student might be doing it, but a less motivated student may rely on the "help" of a parent, friend, or tutor.

If experienced teachers love packets, it probably means their packets feel effective. Teachers may rely on them for an evidence-based grade; after all, packets can easily be used during a parent conference to show diligent completion or mastery of skill-and-drill concepts. In addition, some teachers believe their job is to teach responsibility, and completion of packets can make a teacher feel that he or she has done just that: *I assigned it, and the responsible students completed it. Those who did not received clear, fair consequences.* Further, many packet-committed teachers use packets for purposes related to classroom management, intervention, and enrichment (*I can have students work quietly on packets while I address other needs in my classroom*). Because some teachers are so deeply entrenched in their packet habit, it can feel impossible to challenge their use. In fact, many principals I know eschew packets but hesitate to take on the delicate task of asking teachers to rethink their role in instruction. As in so many cases, dealing with the issue comes down to asking good questions and supporting alternative ways of thinking. If a principal wants to have a solid legacy to brag about, being the catalyst for becoming a packet-less school ranks pretty high on the list.

Reconsider Homework

Before we dig too deeply into this controversial and impassioned topic, let's consider a couple of caveats. First, many of the points made here have more applicability the younger a student is. Second, this section is simply meant to reassess the value and intention behind a teacher's homework philosophy.

In the early years of my teaching career, I was probably the biggest homework fan ever. I assigned it, I graded it, and I punished students who didn't do it. I thought that's what good teachers *did*. I had complex formulas for "points" and "credit." Students who turned in homework one day late lost 25 percent of their points; if it was two days late, they lost 50 percent; if it was late but correct, they received full credit with a parent signature; if it was late but incorrect, they received 50 percent credit with a parent signature. My classroom homework policies were an exhausting and complicated set of rules, standards, and expectations—and *had no connection to student learning*. I don't think I ever stopped to think about *why* I was doing any of it.

That would come, fortunately, because many smart people had begun to think about it—in earnest.

A quick Google search will give a week's worth of reading about the pros and cons of homework. There are research-based articles as well as many emotionally charged viewpoints from people in every area of the educational experience. Reading articles and summations about homework introduces many excellent questions, starting with *why?* Why do we assign homework? Why do some students and parents hate it and others love it? How does the home environment affect homework's role in school? Why do we grade homework? Why might we not grade homework? Most of all, why is it so hard to break out of the confines of traditional homework?

In my case, answering these questions launched some deep self-reflection and led me to radically change my beliefs about the issue, spurred by reading, research, and the perspective-exploding experience of becoming a parent. I learned that homework has little value educationally and that it's only when there is a specific, instructionally supported *intention* behind homework—and communication with the student about that intention—that homework becomes helpful. My reading left me eager to lead a big shift in how and why we use homework.

I knew I couldn't smack down a mandate or alter "policy," nor did I wish to. Local boards of education are the only entity that can adopt or alter a district's policies and procedures. Our district's homework policy was wisely and intentionally vague, essentially leaving homework decisions up to teachers. My only goal was for teachers to make an informed, intention-based decision about the role homework would have in their classrooms.

So we started talking about it, first with a teacher-leader group and then with grade-level departments. Here's how we went about the conversation:

- We did what I called an "article walk," with teachers seeking out various opinions and research about homework and sharing it with colleagues during PLC (professional learning community) time.
- We talked about our intention and purpose when assigning homework.
- We shared successes with homework—solid examples of times students had genuinely showed improvement because of time spent working at home.
- We vented about frustrations with homework, including finding applicable resources, managing the assignment and collection of homework, and determining what homework we should count toward a grade.
- We shared tips and tricks about communication with parents regarding homework.
- We talked about some of our experiences as parents trying to support our own children with homework.

We marveled at the range of emotions and beliefs we had about homework, especially when we told stories based on memories of homework when we, ourselves, had been young students. Some remembered long, angst-filled evenings sequestered at the kitchen table, books scattered around and a harried parent barking about completion. Others remembered a welcome quiet time, working in a pleasant and methodical way.

I told them my own story as a student—of hours spent memorizing spelling words and remembering them just long enough to regurgitate on a test. I remember tears plopping on my algebra homework, my stomach in knots from the anxiety that comes from not knowing how to do something and being fully aware that my diligent completion had developed exactly zero genuinely helpful study skills.

When I was done, someone remarked, "You hate homework, don't you?"

"No," I said. "I hate homework *with no worth.*"

Someone else suggested, "Maybe we shouldn't be thinking about homework as a 'policy.' Maybe we should think of it as a 'philosophy.'"

Ah, yes. But talking about homework as a philosophy made our teachers nervous. Many of them based a great portion of their students' grades on homework, and they felt they needed something tangible, standardized, and predictable to score and grade. Many had their actual identity as a teacher tied up with homework—if they assigned quality homework, they must be a quality teacher, right? And many were hung up on the idea that it was their job to "teach responsibility." They thought homework did just that.

I understood their hesitation. But in the spirit of evolution and risk taking, we dug in anyway, together, having many long and impassioned conversations about our "why" with homework. Here are our conclusions:

- Sometimes completed homework assignments are overseen or even completed by heavily involved parents.
- When there is no parental guidance at home to complete homework, students can be left to their own devices to understand and complete assigned work. Again, this creates a problematic divide between students who have support and those who don't. We end up negatively judging the students who need our help the most.

- By assigning homework, we risk taking time away from student options for immersion learning or reading for pleasure.
- We might get as much value from assigning a couple of rich practice exercises as from multiple pages of practice.
- When teachers claim their homework "teaches responsibility," they are hoping students will write down assignments, prioritize homework during their out-of-school hours, complete all tasks, and turn assignments in, all in the name of being responsible. Does that really teach responsibility, or does it simply reward students who are focused and organized while penalizing students who have challenges related to language, learning, or executive functions?
- When homework is too difficult, is too easy, or seems to be silly busywork, it doesn't promote understanding or enhance content. Instead, it teaches our students that schoolwork can really stink.
- Some teachers don't grade the homework but just offer it as "practice" that the student can choose to complete. But it doesn't take a child long to wonder, "Well, then, why do it?" Students face a dilemma: *I can please my teacher, obey my parent, be a diligent student—or go outside, play with my friends, play video games, do other things.* That seems to me a pretty miserable choice to offer young learners.
- Many teachers vastly underestimate the time it takes to complete an assignment. For example, they may assume the short nonfiction article they've sent home, along with the accompanying comprehension questions, will take 10 minutes to read and complete. But after a long day of school, activities, dinner, and chores, it can take an exhausted child much longer to slog through. In some cases, particularly with younger students, homework involves tears, frustration, and battles between parent and child. This is not the way we want our learners to end their days, nor is it the way we want children to interact with their families.
- Research shows that homework has almost no positive effect on student achievement at the elementary school level. In his

fabulous book *Visible Learning,* John Hattie (2009) points to a study by Cooper, Lindsay, Nye, and Greathouse (1998) that estimated a correlation of near zero between time spent on homework and achievement. Although some positive effects of homework are seen at the junior high and high school level ("twice as large for high as for junior high," according to Cooper and colleagues), that outcome depends on the nature of the homework. Math homework yields the highest effect, and science and social studies homework yields the lowest.

Hattie points out,

> The effects [of homework] are greater for higher than for lower ability students and for older rather than younger students. For too many students, homework reinforces that they cannot learn by themselves, and that they cannot do the schoolwork. For these students, homework can undermine motivation, internalize incorrect routines and strategies, and reinforce less effective study habits, especially for elementary students. (2009, p. 235)

- Some parents judge the effectiveness of schools by the amount of homework assigned—an unfair and misguided view that complicates and perpetuates misunderstandings about homework.
- Strong teachers ask students to work very hard while they are at school. Rigor has increased, testing has increased, and expectations have increased. If we work them hard enough in the seven or eight hours we have them, would it perhaps be all right if they didn't have additional hours of work after school?

As our staff dug into redefining our understanding of homework, most teachers shifted their thinking and greatly adjusted the number and outcome of their assignments. Many teachers eliminated homework altogether, instead simply encouraging students to read, read, read. (Also noteworthy was our extensive discussion of reading logs, another outdated and ineffective "teaching" practice; the discussion led us to stop attempting to monitor student reading time, reward strong readers, or punish absence of reading.) Teachers planned to discuss this fresh and brave new approach to homework at the start of a school year during our annual Parent Night event, explaining our philosophy and the ensuing dial-back on the volume of homework we would assign.

Although we were now pretty solid on our stance on homework, we were anxious about this "parent" step. We practiced what we'd say and how we would answer the inevitable questions. Afterward, we were mostly buoyed by validation: the majority of our parents whooped with joy upon hearing that their children wouldn't have significant nightly homework, if any at all. A select few were shocked and dismayed, particularly parents who had been raised in an environment or culture that valued homework. A couple of teachers found themselves in uncomfortable situations, fielding questions from aggressive parents who disagreed with the teachers' explanations. Afterward, those teachers approached me and asked, "How do we manage parents who insist on more homework?"

"The same way we manage students who have different needs, interests, and goals," I told them. That's just what we did. Some parents benefited from a one-on-one parent-teacher conversation to explain our philosophy. For those who still didn't buy or embrace our approach, we reminded them that there were many online resources available, the best of which were linked on our school website. We also encouraged parents to think of ways to enrich and support their child through music, theater, art, movement and physical challenges, charitable activities, and so on. Those experiences, we reassured them, would be built upon in the classroom and would enrich the learning experience in ways traditional homework could not.

One or two still didn't appreciate or accept our lightened emphasis on homework. One even took to social media, inaccurately describing our philosophy and declaring it "irresponsible." Fortunately, almost all commenters disagreed with the original poster and supported our vision. In the end, the bold step we'd taken proved to be a culture-builder for our staff, students, and most of our parents.

Take a Critical Look at Vendor-Based Programs

If we really believe that differentiation is important, it's difficult to support vendor-based curricular or classroom management programs. Although they may appear to be leveled according to particular summative end-of-unit assessments, or the attainment of particular awards and incentives, they can't and don't take into account the base factors of good differentiated instruction: relationship building, the emotional component of learning, varied motivational tactics and tools, and personalized goal setting.

There are, of course, excellent vendor-based intervention programs, but they shouldn't have unmitigated implementation. Said another way, the purchase of consumables, workbooks, online texts, or subscription-based resources cannot replace good teaching. It can certainly *supplement* good teaching, but principals are fooling themselves if they think the purchase of a resource will ensure student growth and achievement in an authentic, sustainable way. The following reasons explain why this is so:

- *They are expensive.* Vendor-based programs rely on a staff of publishers, sales staff, trainers, and marketers—all of whom need to be paid. Given the steep cost, purchasing a vendor-based program means a financial investment for many years. What would happen if all that money were invested instead in meaningful professional development that increased teacher efficacy, confidence, and innovation?

- *Most aren't consistent over time.* Sustainability of vendor-based programs depends on their sales, and sales depend on their staff longevity. The fastest way for a principal to ensure teachers' disillusionment is to insist they accept and implement a program and then have to break the news that the program isn't sustainable. It may have become too expensive, been proven to be ineffective, or even gone defunct.

- *Most lack attention to diversity and student input.* Vendor-based programs tend to do a poor job matching students with resources that reflect the students' own experiences, and they offer little to no student choice and virtually no opportunity for the sharing of student voice. No choice and voice? No good.

- *Many sprout from buzzwords and related marketing.* Type *STEM* or *STEAM* or *blended learning* or *literacy* into an online search, and you'll be inundated with options for what you can buy. Just like beautiful graphics on an online tool, though, careful placement of buzzwords doesn't indicate good resources for teaching.

Embracing the New

When she was younger, my daughter and I worked our way through Laura Ingalls Wilder's *Little House* series. I'd read the series as a child and remembered being fascinated with stories of Laura as a student and then later, when she is hired as a teacher. Reading it aloud decades later, I was again enraptured by Wilder's descriptions of how classrooms were managed and what was expected of students. This time, though, I read them through the lens of a school principal and was struck by how much the school experience has evolved in remarkable ways since Laura's experience in the 19th century, as has the management of discipline, the extensive use of resources, and the size and scope of our schools. Some of the changes are due to societal and population changes (few of us teach in a sparsely populated prairie environment and wear bonnets to work), but others result from an increased focus on the individual student. Thank goodness!

And we're still evolving—or, at least, we should be.

A colleague and I met recently to work on a teacher evaluation I'd been struggling with. The teacher was doing everything just fine, but I found zero inspiration or energy in her teaching. I'd wondered if my apathy came from me—an indicator of some sort of approaching demise to my effectiveness as a principal—or if I needed to push this teacher to evolve in her classroom practices. My colleague offered to meet with me to talk about ways to make the evaluation worthwhile for both me and the teacher. Out of the blue, he asked a seemingly unrelated question: "I wonder what schools will look like in the 22nd century?"

But it *wasn't* an unrelated question. It was more relevant to the issue than anything we'd discussed thus far, taking a longer view than most of the thinking we do about school. What if I approached the evaluation conversation by wondering what her classroom should look like not today, but in 10 years, in 20, or more? As a principal, I usually feel like I'm just trying to keep up. Teachers feel the same way. But what if our vision extended far into the future? That is the question that drives me now. Rather than ruminating on how and why things have changed in the past, it helps to wonder: *How will things be generations from now, if the brave and smart and strong leaders insist that we evolve the school experience for our students?* The following sections elaborate on a few ways to embrace the new.

Foster New Teaching Strategies

I love when teachers try new instructional practices, and I love to be the person to encourage their doing so. When that happens, I try to make special note of it and talk through their motivations, intentions, and eventual outcomes. I find it exciting to be part of these conversations, especially because it challenges me to be a more cutting-edge leader, but I also like how it validates and frees teachers to be risk takers. If they know they have my full support, they have no roadblocks to slow them down.

Discourage Tendencies to Give Up Too Soon

By my unscientific count, it seems to take teachers around three weeks to grow comfortable with a new classroom initiative. It follows, then, that if an effort is abandoned because a one-day attempt didn't unfold smoothly, it is an unfortunate loss for everyone.

A friend of mine was one of the first in her high school history department to try a workshop model unit. After the first day, she announced that such an approach would never work in high school because there was too much information to cover, which meant direct lecture-based instruction was really the only way. Fortunately, her principal encouraged her to stick with it. "All those workshop disciples can't be wrong, can they?" she asked. "We're all watching you, and I, for one, would think it pretty awesome if it worked out well." So my friend stuck with it, and a month later, she announced she'd never go back to the traditional model of teaching. Her history classes had evolved from "sit-and-git" lectures to small-group, interest-based research; blended learning; and differentiation—and, yes, more content than she could cover in three months using her previous teaching style.

Set Up a System of Peer Modeling and Feedback

Try as we might, principals simply can't be everywhere and see everything. So although I want them to try new things, I can't be every teacher's individual cheerleader and muse; there are too many of them and too few of me. That's why a peer observation program can be so effective, especially if it follows an all-doors-open culture in which teachers help one another cover classes, provide before-and-after debriefing to discuss intentionality and outcomes, and celebrate collegial risk taking.

Note that a principal doesn't have to—indeed, shouldn't—initiate or micromanage a peer observation program; instead, the principal should trust the enthusiastic leaders behind the idea and come from a place of yes. "Is it OK if I go observe another classroom while my students are in a combined class with my team teacher?" Yes. "May I have a professional release day to spend time in a couple of classrooms in a nearby 'sister' building?" Yes. "Are you OK with me hosting some other teachers in my room?" Yes, yes, yes.

In our district, instructional coaches own the peer feedback system. They developed a "collaborative classroom" approach in which (with principal approval) teachers request a visit to another classroom. The coaches are the catalyst for it all, and I don't believe it would be effective without their leadership. They set up the visit, provide probing questions for the host teacher and the visitor, and send me a brief recap afterward. I always approve these requests, figuring they are far more valuable than most other professional development requests I receive. After I stamp my approval, though, I get—and stay—out of the way, eagerly awaiting the recap.

Noteworthy here is the value teachers can find observing a lesson from a teacher in an entirely different age group and content area. Middle school science teachers might observe a high school English teacher. A 6th grade language arts teacher might visit a small-group reading instructor. Good instruction knows no age or content boundaries, and it can be eye-opening and inspiring for teachers to jump completely out of their knowledge area and see good instruction at work in other ways. I try to tag along on these sorts of visits whenever I can. Last year, I observed a high school English teacher—returning to my roots, if you will, though I hadn't been in an advanced English class in decades. I walked on a pink cloud for days afterward, brimming with ideas and inspiration—and I'm not even, officially, a teacher. But the ideas and energy of good teaching absolutely apply to my principal work.

Establish a Teacher Learning Lab

Wouldn't it be fun to create a teacher-created, teacher-led, teacher-managed space that can wield more school culture punch than the teachers' lounge? That's not to say the lounge should be abandoned; after all, there are some things you just don't touch. But if there were a place where teachers would want to go to share resources, frustrations, and ideas, it could grow into a powerful place for teachers to learn, just as a library or learning lab does for students. The instructional coach could be based there, as could some new and applicable books and online learning tools. At the beginning, there may need to be incentives for teachers to visit the lab, such as rewards or instructional resources as gifts (or notations in the "professionalism" area on the teacher evaluation rubric), but if time spent in the lab offers real-life value, it could grow into something unique and innovative for teachers.

Encourage Displays and Documentation of Progress

Documenting student growth goes beyond well-appointed bulletin boards or posters with inspirational quotes. There is value in these (who *hasn't* spent time daydreaming and gazing at a teacher's posters and ruminating on their meaning?), but they don't reflect student learning journeys. Instead, principals can encourage student-led and student-created evidence of learning. I love seeing a display of student learning in which it is clear the teacher didn't intervene but instead let the students drive the purpose and product. This documentation includes student presentations, digital portfolios, performances, writing journals, Readers Theater, and so on.

Support Project-Based Learning

Much has been written about project-based learning, and there are countless examples, from mini to mammoth, with students young and not so young. It can feel risky for a teacher to adopt this sort of philosophy, especially because it can require a *lot* of work on the teacher's part. A friend of mine recently launched her first project-based learning experiment, and she was swamped by the role she needed to play in all the student projects—helping link students with community members, planning culminating presentations or experiences, communicating with colleagues and parents and various other stakeholders. But in the end, she was grateful she'd taken the risk and put in the hard work, because her students had gained learning and experience on a level far beyond her previous practice of having them read an article and write a paper. She vowed to continue to base her instruction on capstone projects, with the caveat that she would grow smarter and more efficient in *her* role leading them. Indeed, she has done just that: like teachers of many successful project-based learning models, she has learned how to step back so her primary role is "chief facilitator," while her students drive the interest, application, and outcome of the projects.

Incorporate Blended Learning and Technology

These aren't new questions, but they're worth revisiting: Is technology something to teach, in and of itself? Or is it a tool to use to accompany teaching? Or both? How well are teachers blending traditional teaching practices with the new tools available to us? With all our other responsibilities, principals can't be the sole trailblazers for finding, vetting, and implementing the use of technology—but we can offer energy and spirit behind legitimate, long-lasting shifts in how teachers think about technology.

My district has done a lot of research and work trying to grasp what we mean by "blended learning." We came up with some questions to help teachers understand the term:

- Is the learning personalized for students?
- Do students have ownership and decision-making capabilities?
- Are there opportunities for connection with other students, locally and around the world, in a safe and focused way?
- Are students able to collaborate in a platform that encourages creativity and innovative thinking?
- Is there a legitimate audience for student work?

I have watched hundreds of "blended learning" classrooms, and I still can't easily identify what blended learning is and what it's not. I once watched an AP Psychology course in which students seemed to be staring at their computers throughout the entire class, occasionally coming to the teacher's desk for a quick conference. The class didn't seem to include blended learning at all. I asked the teacher about it. He explained a multiday process in which students took on a case study, researched components, provided alternate inputs and perspectives, and then compiled their learning in an online "society" they'd created. They would eventually present their work to a visiting psychology professor at a nearby community college. I felt awestruck, if a bit chastised. It appeared the unit was an exemplary blended learning experience. Armed with knowledge and perspective, I went back to observe the presentations and saw all the components I'd missed the first time—personalization, presentation, and purpose.

By contrast, I've seen lessons in which students are working alone at seek-and-click online activities with little to no interaction with others and virtually no long-lasting learning, but an "end product" the teacher can score and enter into a grading system. As in our previous discussion of packets, it's easy to assume any activity with an end point and a gradable product is a quality activity. How can we know for sure? For principals, the key is to avoid quick-fire judgments that might give teachers pause or make them scared to try new things. We can ask questions about rationale and encourage teachers to rely on one another in the development and debriefing of blended learning experiences. We can also remember that there will be duds, but there will also be darlings. Blended learning is a brave new world, but a principal can be at the forefront of the journey and find a great deal of inspiration revamping how we "do" technology in our schools.

Rethink Learning Spaces

I've attended professional development sessions in which we all dream big about what learning spaces can and should look like. I always walk out of those sessions a little depressed, because my dreams are in complete conflict with what I am actually permitted to do. Principals don't have the power to raze buildings, tear down walls, or fund complete furniture overhauls. We mostly have to make do with what we have.

The thing we *can* do? Challenge teachers to think differently about learning spaces, and put our support behind their ideas. What if teachers want to try some flexible seating in their classrooms? What about flexible grouping, outdoor classrooms, alternative classrooms, small-group and conferring setups, and nontraditional furniture? Yes, I say. Yes, yes, yes. If there is a rationale, if there is a plan, and if there is a tool to monitor effectiveness and positive outcome, I'm all in.

I'm a big believer in freshening things up by having teachers move classrooms within a building, too—not that it's easy. Teachers are infamous for their reluctance to change classrooms in any capacity. Last year, we were facing some overcrowding issues, so I had to ask a teacher to move after she'd spent 17 years in one room. She was incensed, though she kept her responses professional (in my presence, anyway). I chirped away about how much she'd thank me in the end, and I was right. Indeed, the teacher had to spend many hours cleaning and purging, and I watched her go from grumpy to embarrassed to humbled by how much *stuff* she had to throw away. The sheer volume of outdated supplies and resources crammed in her storage spaces forced her to think carefully about what she really needed in this 21st century world—and what she didn't. It drove her to reflect on how she'd changed as a teacher. In the end, she found new zest and vigor in her new learning environment, and so did I, just by watching. Imagine how her students felt.

Ask for Innovation

I once worked with a superintendent who didn't fear change; in fact, he craved it. At one point, he and our school treasurer allocated a sum of money to award grants to teachers who wanted to take on some innovative practices. I was lucky enough to find myself on the committee to develop standards and qualifications for the grants. We had a great time thinking big and broad. In the end, we developed an application with the following elements:

- Any staff member could apply (including certified, classified, and support staff).
- Ideas had to embrace an innovative instructional practice with an eye to improving student achievement and enhancing learning environments.
- Applicants had to create a short video introduction outlining their plans, incorporating the following requirements:
  - Plans for sustainability beyond the grant time line
  - Abiding by district purchasing and procurement procedures
  - Being willing to serve as a model/mentor for future grant recipients

After reviewing and voting on their ideas, we would allocate money to successful applicants and offer additional support, including the following:

- Time for planning (including subs for release time)
- Space for planning as needed
- Technology support
- A design coach to help with developing ideas

We intentionally kept our criteria vague, because we didn't want our preconceived ideas of "innovation" to constrain us. We wanted to encourage—without limits. It was great fun to hear some of the ideas put forth by teachers and so exciting to imagine the impact their courageous thinking and hard work would have on students. The effort grew into one of the most energizing projects I'd done as a principal because it sparked innovation in my own mind; I reevaluated some of our school's old, tired instructional practices and dabbled in the possibilities for novel ones.

There's no better way to get innovation than to ask for it. Why not throw out the challenge to teachers, asking them to think about what they'd love to do if there were no constraints on them? Why not make your school a place where new ideas are supported and celebrated? And as for financial support, if you don't have district funding to support innovation in the classroom, it might be a refreshing and welcome challenge to find ways to allocate your building budget to fund this type of work. Other sources of monies, such as parent-teacher organizations, community groups, or alumni support, may bolster your options, as would grants or other funding from corporate sponsors and partnerships.

● ● ●

As we discussed at the beginning of this chapter, principals can so easily grow weary and worn by the responsibility of being a school's sole instructional leader, especially if current instructional practices are weary and worn. There's no better way to reboot than by evaluating how instruction really looks in our schools and considering how teachers and students alike would benefit by purging outdated practices, providing opportunities for risk taking, and developing a culture of innovative thinking. Principals can find great energy by supporting unique thought and revamping approaches to teaching. There really are no limits —and what could be more exciting than that?

Reenvision Teacher Potential: Catching the Growing Wave of Teacher Leadership

What's a great way for principals to reboot? Stop *doing* everything. That doesn't mean intentionally neglecting responsibilities—quite the opposite, actually. It means reenvisioning what leadership looks like and taking action so the entire weight of a building's success doesn't fall on the shoulders of one person.

I had a friend who was the principal of a large, high-pressure high school. For years, she worked upward of 70 hours a week. She was always at school, always present, always available. She retired to great fanfare, feeling proud and accomplished as she handed the keys to her successor, one of her assistant principals whom she'd mentored for several years. The two were close friends and met for coffee every couple of months. Late in January of his first year as principal, she asked how he was holding up under the soul-crushing weight of a 70-hour-a-week job. He shrugged, a little sheepish, and admitted he averaged about 50 hours a week.

She was incredulous.

"I don't try to do it all, like you did," he said. "I know I can't sustain that type of pace."

"But . . . 50 hours? *How?*"

"I utilize the assistants to their capacity, but I also rely heavily on the teachers." He purposefully delegated tasks by challenging teachers to take leadership roles. He found creative ways to "compensate" teachers for time-intensive roles, such as reallocating duties and providing occasional sub support, and even advocated for additional board-approved stipends for several teachers to become designated "facility managers" for evening events. His most effective step, though, was more philosophical than managerial: he respectfully refused to get involved in situations he knew could be handled perfectly well by someone else.

My friend struggled to reconcile her "legacy" with the reality of the school's new leadership. At first, she was despondent, regretful, and even angry. She had been so very proud of her identity as *the hardest worker.* That's what she thought a principal should be. She attended every event. She answered every call that came her way. She personally managed all difficult or intensive staffing or parent problems. She attended every meeting possible, and when a conflict kept her away, she requested detailed meeting minutes and read them exhaustively. She had a great team of three assistant principals but primarily relied on them for managing standard discipline procedures, special education, and facility decisions. But even when they were in charge, she insisted on regular debriefs, and ultimately it was she who approved all decisions. Did she have the assistants cover evening events? Sure—but she attended them, too.

Then along came this guy who demonstrated she hadn't needed to be everyone's everything.

Indeed, it *had* been a shift in mindset for the school community when he'd come on the scene and not been so omnipresent. Some people, of course, grumbled and questioned his commitment, complaining when he had his secretary answer his phone and manage his calendar, sniffing when he didn't attend every single after-school and evening event. He stayed the course, though, boldly articulating that it was actually his goal to *not* oversee every issue at the school.

He felt it was his job to find ways to share leadership opportunities and give credit to the contributions of others. Soon others began to accept their new normal, and most even celebrated, kicking up their heels with a feeling of both emancipation and empowerment.

My now-retired friend has reconciled her legacy with the new principal's leadership style, understanding the fundamental differences between the two. She recognizes that her legacy does still matter—a lot—and people love and respect her and admire her tireless work for their school. She now knows, though (too late, unfortunately), that she didn't have to own every little detail or work so hard to gain professional respect and admiration.

It may be too late for her to change her approach, but it's not too late for us. We can look around, recognize the army that surrounds us, and let it take over much of the job. By doing so, we will find professional energy and accomplishment in the delegation and distribution of work to teachers—in other words, in letting teacher leadership be a defining component of our professional identity while saving ourselves from inevitable burnout.

This chapter is divided into four sections related to teacher potential and leadership. The first concerns how principals can find new energy and purpose by relinquishing control and allowing teachers to take on decision-making and leadership responsibilities. The second explores how to identify teachers with the skill and know-how to help lead. The third delineates eight areas in which teachers might excel as leaders, and the fourth looks at how principals can support and mentor them.

Why Shared Leadership?

We've all heard it: "Great leaders hire great people and then get out of their way." I'd adjust the phrase slightly to say, "Great principals hire good people, support their growth, find opportunities for them, and cheer like crazy when they, too, begin to lead." I would also adjust it to say, "Great leaders don't think so highly of themselves—or so little of others—that they don't trust anyone else to lead."

It's not easy to let go, especially if, somewhere along the way, the idea was planted in our minds that a good principal should oversee every single thing. It's also a real risk for people like me, because I have that "people pleaser" gene that makes me want to be everyone's hero, swooping in to save the day. And if I'm honest, I admit it: I like getting the credit for excellence. Of course I do. Don't we all?

So why let go of control? Why share leadership with teachers and staff? Here's why.

It's a long career. Especially for those of us who started on the administrator path early in our career, being the type of principal who insists on having a hand in every little thing isn't tenable for the long haul. It takes too much out of us over time. A school will suck up every ounce of time and energy the principal gives; it's up to us to decide what—and how much—we offer up. If we're spread too thin or feeling overwhelmed, the only reprieve is to get help so we can keep our energy and enthusiasm at sustainable levels.

Teachers are skilled at what they do. Really—they are. For the purposes of this conversation, let's assume we're talking about our high-quality teachers, not the teachers on improvement plans or those we have to motivate with constant supervision. Strong teachers are, by nature, leaders, even if on a smaller scale. They tend to be planners and doers, organized and articulate. They can command the attention and buy-in of students as they deliver insight, inspiration, and information. If that's not a leader, I don't know what is.

Teachers thrive on challenge and acknowledgment. Even skilled teachers can be overlooked and underused outside their classrooms. In fact, sometimes the best potential leaders are unintentionally slighted or unappreciated. To acknowledge their talents by having them take the lead on something is the highest compliment we can bestow. It's a way of saying, "You're really good, and I trust you." It's a win-win situation: they get acknowledgment and confidence; we get help.

Helpers increase efficiency. "Many hands make light work," said our grandmothers. They were right. When we have other people helping clean house, the work isn't easier, but it's distributed among many, so it *feels* easier. Having help also eliminates the need for the principal to be running around like the house is on fire, pointing the fire extinguisher willy-nilly at random flames. Instead, there are more stakeholders and more people who want the work done well.

Sharing improves community and culture. A reverse effect occurs when a principal insists on micromanaging. Far from being a revered monarch on the throne, the principal becomes overextended and begins to drop things, forget things, and appear ineffective. Teachers take notice, get annoyed, lose faith, and, in an attempt at self-preservation, disengage. They do *that thing:* "I'm going to close my classroom door and just teach—by myself." Positive culture tanks. Standing alone is the principal—working tirelessly, trying to have a hand in everything, and feeling exhausted and baffled as to why it's all happening. It's these situations that give the principalship its reputation as a lonely job.

On the flip side, when we let go of control and invite others to join the work, trust and valuation become the norm. Teachers and support staff are invested and take ownership of the school's success. Happy teachers lead to a strong school culture, which leads to a positive workplace, which leads to an effective school, which leads to a happy principal. A relieved principal. An "I can keep doing this" principal.

Shared leadership enables instructional mastery. I don't mind admitting that I do not (and cannot) know every standard, every nuance of curriculum, every material or supplemental resource available at every grade level. My school is too big and there are too many other responsibilities for me to manage. That's why I count on teacher leaders to be the curricular masters for our school. They clarify and deconstruct standards, suggest how to approach instruction, and provide professional development for other teachers. If I have a question about how, when, and to what extent a concept should be taught in a classroom, or if I wonder how curricular decisions fit into the larger scope of our school's work, I find my way to a teacher—one who is thriving as a reputable, innovative, skilled instructional leader. Teachers are our practitioners and specialists; they do the daily work that affects students, parents, and the colleagues that surround them. Why wouldn't I want to let these types of professionals be leaders in our school?

Identifying Leadership Potential

Even longtime principals can grow blind to the supplementary talents of teachers. It is easy to miss rising restlessness. Teachers might be bubbling over with potential, but from our perspective, if everything feels steady and solid and there are no surface issues to address, we may overlook the possibilities. We just keep doing the same thing and expecting the same output from our teachers, year after year. But as we reenvision teacher leadership, we'll need to actively seek teachers who want to be more visible in their leadership. As part of that process, we need to identify what skills they carry and how they could contribute to school decisions and direction.

Doing so is not always easy. As suggested earlier, when we discuss teacher leadership, we're assuming that the teachers we empower as leaders are, first and foremost, excellent teachers. Let's also acknowledge that being a strong teacher doesn't necessarily indicate that someone is an obvious leader. Or, perhaps better said, some teachers might be leaders, but in a quiet or unassuming way. I often think of a teacher I know who is a true master in the classroom. She is a leader *because of* her excellence, not *in addition to* it. In fact, she would never want to be an outspoken or official leader; it's not in her nature. Instead, she wants to keep being a masterful teacher without being pointed out. She likes working in small settings and as a quiet consultant on any issues related to curriculum and instruction, but she demurs when asked to step up and lead in a more formalized way. That's fine, of course; I love her for the teacher she is, because her leadership style contributes to our school's particular needs.

Indeed, sometimes those hidden gems are the ones we need to find. They don't necessarily fit the stereotypes. They may not be the most experienced, the most verbal, or the most aggressive. They are leaders, though, of the finest type.

Several years ago, I needed a teacher to step up and join a districtwide committee that would be auditing, adjusting, and adopting a new math curriculum. It had to be someone who was (or could become) an expert in mathematics instruction, someone who had the backbone to stand tall and deliver an informed decision. The person also had to have eloquence in justifying and explaining the new math program and supporting teachers when it rolled out at the building level.

Anita was just in her third year of teaching, but I knew she'd be perfect. I approached her about the opportunity. She was taken aback. "I'm a third-year teacher," she said hesitantly. "I feel like I don't have the necessary expertise."

"You'll learn everything you need to learn," I reassured her. "Far more important are your natural, innate skills that can't easily be taught. There are teachers with decades of experience who don't have an intrinsic ability to lead, and I already see it in you." What I meant was that, even after working with her for just a couple of years, I'd seen the following traits:

- Commitment to her craft
- Philosophical grounding in instructional strategies
- Willingness to learn
- Work ethic
- Collegial support and respect
- Ability to "read a room"
- Perspective and eye on the long road
- Confidence
- Communication skills, including active listening and clear, concise delivery
- Patience
- Purpose
- Naturally, relentlessly positive attitude

With my vote of confidence, Anita agreed to serve on the district committee. It was a lot of work and took many months. As the process wrapped up and the board of education voted on the final curriculum decision, our director of curriculum called to rave about Anita, telling me, "She was instrumental in this process. It's great you took a chance on such a young teacher. She was far better than some of the veteran teachers on the committee." From my view at the school level, I enthusiastically concurred. She had been everything I'd hoped she'd be—and more—as she communicated with the rest of the staff, provided training, and distributed resources. She's still serving in her leadership position today, growing and offering input on mathematics instruction at the state level through participation in workgroups and committees. She has even presented at notable math conferences and is considering writing articles on mathematics instruction.

If you have teachers with some of the skills listed above, it's almost a professional duty to tap them and share their greatness with other educators. Give them the steering wheel and let them drive. They can do it, and the whole school community will be better for it.

How do you do this? Here are a few ideas to think about as you communicate with teachers, either in informal conversations that occur next to the microwave in the lounge or in more formal evaluation conferences.

Share your confidence in them. I may never have taken leadership steps in my career without a principal who believed in me *and told me so.* "I know you are going to do something special in the world of education," she told me. At the time, I didn't trust her prediction —perhaps I still don't—but I was so buoyed by her vote of confidence that I felt obligated to put on my bravest face, consider myself a potential leader, and take a few key risks. She put me in positions to lead, and I jumped on every chance because I knew she knew I could do it, and I wanted to make her proud.

Ask about their professional goals. In addition to discussing the great work they do in the classroom, I love talking with teachers about what's next. Again, this is sometimes an informal process in which I take advantage of a conversation that lends itself to discussions of the future; other times, it's a spin-off from a postobservation conference. If teachers don't know what they'd like to do, I offer ideas and suggestions. The world of education is full of opportunities, and sometimes the principal has a perspective the teacher may not have considered. We all have dreams, and I love hearing about teachers' aspirations—especially if I can do something to help.

Consider your school's needs. Having reenvisioned your school's processes with teacher leadership, and knowing what leadership skills and professional wishes exist among your staff, it is time to reconcile the two by asking the following questions: *How can teachers lead in a way that benefits the school? Where do you need help? Is there something you hate doing, something you know you don't do well? Is there someone who might love doing it and could take it to a level of excellence you hadn't considered? Is there a way your school's vision and mission might be bolstered and brightened with input from a teacher leader?*

Take on a big project, and humbly ask for help. This book is full of ideas for how to reboot your work as a principal, which, of course, is also a reboot for your school, teachers, and students. If there is a project or challenge you're taking on, look around and see what you need and who can fill that need.

Get out of the way. My husband and I jokingly say to each other—in the way that some jokes are actually based in seriousness—*You can't ask me to do something and then criticize how I do it.* Similarly, when you give teachers the opportunity to take control over a component of your school's mission, you've got to let them do it without criticism, input, or constant oversight. Will there be blunders? Absolutely. Missteps and mistakes? Certainly. The job won't be done how you would do it, but that's the beautiful thing about shared leadership: you can let go, be there to provide support if it's needed, and lead the celebration when it's done well.

Cast a wide net. In reaching for teachers to grow into leaders, it doesn't hurt to cast the net to the entire staff by articulating your vision in broad terms. I consider this a sign of strength for a principal, especially if it comes with thorough explanations of democracy and teamwork, because it conveys wisdom and humility. Articulating your desire to delegate and authorize staff to make decisions helps them see your vision and step up to help with it. And it might uncover leaders you hadn't known were there, available and ready to jump in to take something over. Just last year we planned a Movie Night event with our PTO, but the date seemed so far in the future that I actually forgot about it until I saw it pop up on my calendar. I panicked. Every hour of my time leading up to the event was spoken for, and I knew I'd bungle it if I tried to plan and manage the whole thing while juggling all my other responsibilities. So at a staff meeting I threw out a plea for help, admitting my oversight: "I suddenly find myself overcommitted and overextended, so I'm really hoping someone can jump in to plan and manage Movie Night." I gave a few details and then moved on to other agenda items. A teacher I'd never considered for the role approached me afterward and told me she'd be happy to take it on. Done. It was that easy.

Eight Areas Where Teachers Can Lead

Too often, I've observed principals who "mentor" teachers toward leadership by suggesting they move into the principalship. It's the path *we* took, so it is familiar and, seemingly, logical. In some cases, it's good advice, but certainly not always; in fact, it can be short-sighted and detrimental to the teacher in question. For one thing, getting administrative certificates is an expensive, long-term endeavor, and if it's not the right path or if the teacher goes through a program and then isn't able to land a job as a principal, the financial and time commitment is wasted and the teacher may grow bitter and resentful about lost chances. Further, it limits how a principal can use staff. If teachers are committed to classwork and internships related to a principalship program, much of their time and energy go to their college or university, not your school. Finally, principal jobs are actually relatively rare. Schools only get one, right? So to encourage someone to join the principalship is absolutely the right thing to do in certain circumstances, but it can't be a universal recommendation. Instead, we can communicate with teachers, identify our needs, and lob ideas back and forth, seeing if the teacher's dreams and direction can go in a path that best fits that teacher at that point in time.

Here are eight areas where teachers can have a leadership impact on your school:

1. Data and assessment. I have a complicated relationship with data and assessment (more on this in Chapter 6), so I am especially grateful for teachers who can help navigate data analysis, presentation, and consideration of next steps. If I have a teacher who loves data and can interpret what a data report might mean for students, I snatch her up and keep her close by. I have a colleague who is the coordinator of data and assessment for a huge neighboring district; she's forgotten more about data than I'll ever know. Where did she begin? As a teacher, fascinated by data reports. Data reports were foreign territory to me, but clearly her destiny.

2. Staff professional development. Here's a universal truth: educators love peer-led professional development. It's difficult for us to sit and get ideas, suggestions, or guidance from someone who isn't immersed in our work or walking in similar shoes every day. I used to think it had to be *me* leading all professional development in my building. I shudder at how wrong I was. Now I rely almost exclusively on teachers to provide professional development to other teachers. We use a proposal-driven, choice-based approach: teachers submit ideas for sessions for our monthly Professional Development Academy, and staff choose among several options. By all measures—anecdotal, survey, attendance, and response—our staff find this model to be beneficial, practical, engaging, and comprehensive. My role? Minimal. Teacher leaders? In charge.

3. Content support, department heads, team leaders. This area of teacher leadership, just like professional development, thrives with involvement by teachers who are exceptionally passionate about their content and firmly rooted in current instructional practices.

4. Technology integration in content. We all know teachers who don't blink when they think about using technology in the classroom or how to troubleshoot problems. They are a stark contrast to teachers for whom technology is a constant hiccup, who feel technology adds a complicated layer to the already overwhelming list of what is expected or required of them. Integrating technology is not natural or easy for many teachers, so it is hard to get reluctant staff on board. We can do just that, though, by relying on the capabilities of tech-savvy teachers. They are the ones who can help the rest of the staff grow knowledgeable and comfortable with tech tools. Technology teacher leaders seem innately curious about how tools can become part of a student's digital learning portfolio over the course of a day, a week, a year, and, indeed, an entire school journey. They are easy to spot, too. They hop up to grab the remote when the projector won't turn on; they volunteer to pilot new software; they seem on a constant search to discover, learn about, and experiment with new products or programs. They naturally identify, diagnose, and repair most problems. There is great value in having a teacher (or better yet, a team of teacher leaders) available to infuse technology into your school's identity.

5. Club advisement, extracurricular activities, or academic/ extracurricular liaison. Schools don't bloom outside the classroom without teachers who pour their energy into nonacademic learning. I once interviewed a teacher who faltered when I explained our teacher-leadership model and asked how she could contribute to our school outside the classroom. Could she coach? No, she wasn't comfortable with anything athletic. Co-advise our writing club? No, that seemed a bit much. Help out with our drama department? Oh goodness, no! Did she have any ideas for how she could support students outside the school day? No, not really, she said. Needless to say, there wasn't a second interview. This was the sort of teacher candidate who not only didn't exhibit leadership skills (or initiative) but also didn't recognize the larger picture of a school, in which we all need to contribute beyond our content areas.

6. Community outreach. I have a teacher who has no desire to take on a formal leadership role, despite my ongoing encouragement. She just loves what she teaches and pours her leadership energy into working with students to connect with the world outside our walls. As of this writing, she had just finished overseeing a community service project in which her students immersed themselves in a retirement community for several months. They visited the home, decorated the common areas for the holidays, read to residents, and performed musical versions of classic songs. It is difficult to quantify the effect this project had on the residents, our students, and the larger community.

7. Political activism, lobbying, or educational advocacy. We've seen a recent uptick in educators seeking and holding political office. It's no wonder. Teachers have a unique view on the implications of political wrangling, in large part because their perspective considers the future *as it will affect our youth*. Moreover, teachers tend to have the necessary eloquence to articulate their position—and garner followers. I relentlessly encourage teachers who get involved in association work, lobbying, or weighing in on political issues. We need the voices of educators to be heard, and I can't think of anyone more qualified or capable than a teacher. A few years ago, our district's union president ran for a state senate seat, and she used her platform to highlight some of the most objectionable practices in education as well as broad-sweeping celebrations and trailblazing accomplishments both in academics and in extracurricular opportunities. It was a brave, bold, and beautiful leadership risk for her to take, and we were all better for it.

8. Mentoring new teachers or student teachers. Before I went into school leadership, I hosted three student teachers. At the time I don't think I consciously articulated my motive in readily agreeing to the responsibility, but looking back, I see it was a way I could learn how to be a leader in a small, safe environment. I could lead, learn, and give something back to the profession I loved so much. All those things happened, *and* I solidified my interest in and philosophy about guiding young adults to build their teaching schema.

Helping teachers grow as leaders is a great deal of fun and brings validation and inspiration, especially if we are stagnant or stuck in the same old, same old. I find energy boosts in providing positive input toward a teacher's professional journey. When I'm gone and teachers are talking about me (and they will), I hope a component of my legacy will be that I helped teachers become their best professional selves. I want teachers to think, "My principal saw potential in me and helped me find and fulfill it." I want to be remembered as someone who gave back to the profession by creating opportunities and lifting teachers to be powerful and influential masters of their craft.

What Principals Can Do

For teacher leadership to gain traction, principals need to have a mindset of selflessness. Intentional and purposeful mentoring means there is no room for ego or credit grabbing. As discussed earlier in this chapter, wise leaders recognize the myriad reasons to share leadership with teachers. With that in mind, let's address some actionable steps principals can take to grow teachers into leaders.

Capitalize on strengths. It is in most principals' nature to constantly and carefully watch teachers as they work. This tendency comes from a "walk-through" mindset. I am always gathering information about teacher strengths and weaknesses, some of which I document in formalized observations and some of which just live in my mind and memory. These mental files are the ones I access when, say, someone asks me to write a recommendation letter, or when I'm asked about that teacher's skills. I also access those files when encouraging teachers to join in an effort that would benefit from their skills. "You have such a way with people; you are simultaneously reassuring and straightforward, so they trust you and want to be part of whatever you're doing," I might say, or "Your organization and follow-through are what have built your reputation as a hardworking, dedicated, and focused member of this staff." Mentioning specific examples gives more teeth to the conversation: "I really enjoy watching you take charge in difficult IEP meetings." "Your paperwork is always completed beautifully, with no errors in your writing or your compilation of data." "You have a gift for explaining complicated systems to parents, especially when they are upset or anxious, and you read their facial expressions and adjust your approach to alleviate their anxiety." Such observations are complimentary and detailed, all at once.

Identify interests. Finding what tickles and trips teachers' triggers is another way to connect with potential leaders. A teacher on my staff did an excellent job in the classroom, and I'd noticed she liked to incentivize and motivate her students with music, dancing, and sassy, energetic interactions. In fact, a popular end-of-term reward in her classroom was when she brought her karaoke machine from home and led students in a sing-off. I asked her about it, and she said she'd always loved dance and music. She had never pursued her love beyond recreational involvement, such as being on her high school cheer-dance team and casual dancing—"and salsa!"—but she just loved the energy that came from group dance and uplifting music. I filed away these little tidbits about her, and when I had the idea to "gift" our students with a staff performance of a popular current dance song the day before holiday break, I went to her for help. She mobilized the rest of the staff, planned the performance, led several rehearsals, and ultimately produced a show that brought our students to their feet. Interest begets passion, and passion begets results.

Help teachers set long-term goals. As part of many teacher evaluation systems, principals collaborate with teachers to write goals. Most of these are short-term, addressing the current year's students or an "immediate" time span of one to three years. Potential teacher leaders sometimes like to broaden that vision, though; they enjoy dreaming big and setting longer-term goals.

Perhaps I'm pointing out the obvious, but I admit I do not do this with everyone. In all honesty, I wouldn't have the time to sit down with every teacher every year and write meaningful goals about their future as educators. Instead, I select just a handful of teachers every year with whom I dig deeper and discuss goals in increments of decades rather than months or years. By *select,* I don't mean that I make this a premeditated choice; rather, I just take advantage of naturally occurring opportunities to extend conversations with teachers who open the door to this type of conversation.

Encourage risk taking. Perhaps the scariest thing about taking a professional risk is the fear that we won't be good at the work, that we've fooled someone into taking a chance on us, and that we'll be revealed for the frauds we are. When we see teachers hesitating to take a professional plunge, they may need a confidence-building nudge: "You'll be successful as a leader in this position because you ____." Insert specific applicable traits, skills, and talents the teacher possesses: "Don't be afraid. You can do it."

Stick around. In my first year of teaching, my principal learned I'd been an athlete in high school and remained actively involved in basketball leagues and running clubs. He encouraged me to fill an opening as a basketball and track coach. He said all the right things: he had confidence in me; our school would benefit from my contributions; the young athletes needed a coach just like me. Honored and flattered, I accepted without hesitation. Then? He seemed to disappear. I barely saw him, and when I did, he didn't ask how things were going. I tried to reassure myself by telling myself that he had such confidence in me that he didn't need to oversee my work, but I knew better. He'd wanted the open positions filled, and once they were, he felt his work was done. What a shame! I badly needed further mentoring and guidance. I'd had to cut players from the basketball team after tryouts and had no way to navigate the fury of the parents whose kids were cut; I wasn't confident in my responses to complaints about playing time or, frankly, how best to communicate, manage, and organize all the components of coaching a team. How I longed for someone to talk to, someone to help me process the challenges I was facing!

When a teacher takes a professional risk, it is a good idea to stick around, particularly at the beginning. That's what good mentors do, no? Provide a nudge, and then be a safety net in case of a fall. Invite conversation, be available to process problems, provide some perspective using stories of your own stumbles, brainstorm solutions, and keep the positivity coming.

Implement structures for accountability partnerships. I first heard the term *accountability partner* several years ago. My assistant principal and I use each other for this role, keeping a professional eye on each other and balancing the scale when one of us goes too far one way, forgets the goal we're working on, or loses sight of the larger picture. I like to encourage teacher leaders to find a wingperson to keep them on track. A teammate, a friend, or a colleague who has similar leadership skills and goals can go a long way toward capitalizing on a goal or a dream.

Let them know you are watching and learning, too. One of the hidden benefits of mentorship is what the mentor learns alongside the mentee. Mentees gain confidence when they know that they, too, are bringing valuable input to the relationship. As teachers take on leadership opportunities and flourish in them, it's great to hear the mentor say, "I would never have approached that problem as you did, but I learned so much watching it play out successfully" or "I learned some new tricks seeing you handle that challenge." I often hear myself say, "When I started taking on leadership roles, I did not have the tact or calm demeanor I see in you." Watching others as they work, especially if they're individuals you're eyeing as partners in your own leadership journey, can be enlightening and inspiring.

Find ways to allow shadowing. When people have a dream, they make certain assumptions about how things will be once the dream is realized. We've all done it and experienced the dismay when reality doesn't match the picture we had created. For that reason, it is a great idea for principals to help teacher-leaders-in-waiting shadow someone who is doing similar work. Shadowing gives a real-world experience, albeit on a lesser scale, that the teacher may need to make an informed decision.

I once worked with a teacher who was pretty convinced that she'd like to try instructional coaching. I provided her with a couple of professional development release days to spend with a coach. She came out of the experience recognizing that she had actually misconstrued the role of an instructional coach and suspected she would struggle with the political savvy necessary to be successful in the role. The experience was eye-opening and saved her from making a career detour she would regret.

Don't push. Life is long. Goals change. Dreams change. Life happens, and responsibilities shift dramatically and unexpectedly. A former teacher of mine talks about the beginning of his career, when he was intent on becoming a superintendent. His planned path was clear: he'd become a principal, then a central office leader, then a superintendent. He went after the goal fiercely, landing his first principal job when he was quite young—right about the time he and his wife began their family. Life decisions took over: settling into a community, navigating the complications of raising a child with special needs, a wife realizing she would not be happy or healthy as a stay-at-home parent—all factors that made changing jobs and "climbing up" an irresponsible and selfish path for him. Over time, he settled into his new reality happily and with gusto. "I've changed from the man who was desperate to be a superintendent," he said. "I'm different now. I don't have the career priorities I did when we first talked."

I have made the mistake of hearing a teacher's dreams and getting invested in them, feeling I have to advocate and mentor the teacher toward their fulfillment. I've grown so invested, in fact, that I'm too much like a parent about it, wearing someone else's ambition on my sleeve. I have missed signals warning me that the dream might be waning. "How are classes coming?" I once asked a teacher who'd shared her dream of someday being a curriculum director. Her response was quiet, subdued, and awkward. She avoided a direct answer. Only with prodding did she reveal that she'd taken a pause on classes but hadn't been sure how to tell me. In such cases, reaching for understanding is a wise choice: "It's OK if goals change. That's how life works. I'll be here, regardless of where life takes you."

Of course, schools offer so many different levels of leadership opportunities that teachers don't necessarily need to choose and stay on a particular path. I think of the situation like that of a college student changing majors. It is far better in the end to find our passion area and the correct fit than to forge ahead toward something that doesn't work.

• • •

A big part of a principal's job is to join teachers in a combined effort to benefit students. This isn't a simple process, which is why teacher leaders are so paramount. Beyond the obvious direct effect on students, relying on teachers to take some of the burden off the principal's shoulders will help sustain and bolster the principal's career and give it the reboot it may sorely need.

Reframe Data: Gaining Fresh Insight into Student Growth and Achievement

Many school districts grapple with how to mitigate the high-pressure, anxiety-inducing implications of standardized testing data in the face of significant but untestable factors such as poverty, trauma, absenteeism, apathy, staff burnout, aging facilities, funding inequities—the list goes on and on. For many principals, data review becomes just another thing to manage, another task box to check—which prevents it from being what it could be: the catalyst to motivate a school toward excellence.

It's time, then, to recalibrate the use of data with an eye toward intention and balance. In this chapter, we will explore how to launch schoolwide conversations about data in ways that inspire teachers to set instructional and learning goals for themselves and their students. We will also discuss ways schools can balance standardized testing data with anecdotal and formative assessment data, and offer suggestions for structured follow-through with teachers.

This chapter is not a data primer. It doesn't break down data definitions or recommend ways to write improvement plans for yourself and your school. That has all been done elsewhere. Instead, this chapter will take a different, fresh look at data. My hope is it will provide perspective and peace of mind, a way to find balance and, perhaps most important, the courage to go back to your true north: advocating for kids—because of and *in spite of* the numbers next to their names.

Data as a Challenge

I've not yet met a principal who doesn't worry about data. It is exhausting, is it not? We worry about what our students are learning and whether it will match up to the tests. We worry about the tests— who created them, whether they are worded to give every student a fair shake, how they are "graded." We worry about when, where, and how the results will roll out and how people will respond. We struggle with our own understanding of data, often concealing our skimpy knowledge and bluffing our way through conversations. We worry that we might reach conclusions that might not be legitimate. Worry, worry, worry. Nonstop.

To add to it, we've all read about school-data scandals involving principals, teachers, or district leaders who have scrubbed numbers or publicized erroneous information, sometimes to reach goals or get a pay raise. Data corruption has occurred in various states and cities, sometimes with extensive media coverage and other times, I suspect, without anyone knowing a thing. I reckon bad decision making is rooted in fear of losing one's job or reputation. Fear leads to overzealous goal setting, which leads to shifting mindsets, which leads to a temptation to lie. Data scandals are perplexing, in the most dismal way, because they reveal an ugly truth. The pressure to produce positive assessment results can drive some educators to lose track of what they're supposed to be doing in the first place: focusing on students and their learning.

Data issues are also complicated by the existence of massive testing companies taking advantage of weary or overwhelmed districts and promising the perfect measure—the perfect test, if you will—to capture student progress and growth, to give teachers tools for planning instruction and talking to parents, and to lift struggling students to a new level of achievement.

As principals, we face a variety of challenges navigating assessment cycles, data collection, action, and reaction. But data play an important role in many aspects of teaching and learning, so it's wise to consider the positive side and make data a primary resource for your school's approach to student achievement.

Embracing Data

Data can serve many purposes in a school. These purposes remind us why principals must—and should—embrace data and make data part of their school's conversations.

Measuring progress and providing answers. We need to be able to see how students are progressing over time—a projection for growth and specific areas for intervention if they don't grow as we'd predicted. Data can provide answers to questions about how well a student is progressing, what his or her areas of strength are, and which concepts or standards need revisiting or reteaching. Further, data can help teachers structure conversations with parents and colleagues.

Holding us accountable. Assessments help us know that teachers are covering the required standards, and they can be mirrors showing us what we've done well and where we need to improve. Assessment blueprints can be the starting point for planning a scope and sequence for an entire year. With consistent assessments and appropriate analysis of results, no one teacher can go rogue and teach whatever and however she wants. Data give us a checks-and-balances system, something to which we can answer, and the scaffolding to know and articulate our rationale for doing what we do.

Even with these pillars to prop us up, data are no good to us unless they spur action, right? And too often, data stymie and stall us. We log on to a data portal, click on "results," and become overwhelmed by all the numbers. I always have a stunned moment of "OK . . . but *now* what?" I struggle to know exactly what to do or where to start. After that initial flash of panic, I remember some actionable responses—clear-cut ways to begin using information gleaned from data reports. Read on for some specific action steps.

Informing a school improvement team. It is hugely helpful to have someone else's eyes look at schoolwide, classwide, or individual data reports. Working alone on the study of data is never good practice, because we can too easily speculate our way to erroneous assumptions. We need other people to join us in asking questions, providing alternative explanations, and helping develop a solid plan. Working as a team also helps avoid a real risk of data analysis: making decisions based on panic. I find it immensely comforting to remember that I am not alone in navigating data waters. We *all* own the data.

Playing a role in Response to Intervention (RTI). Strong RTI systems and processes rely on all sorts of data. Standardized assessment data, trend data, progress-monitoring data, indicators drawn from probes and formative assessment data—they all have a role in how we keep an eye on student growth and achievement. So, too, do data points related to attendance, discipline, social-emotional stability, and so on.

Monitoring special education. Further on in this chapter, we will discuss a few alternative ideas for how to reframe special education data, but the topic deserves mention here, too, because strong special education programs rely on data to track student growth, report progress, and make instructional decisions. When intervention specialists, instructional paraprofessionals, and teachers all adopt this foundation, they can be remarkably effective in using data to help their program flourish.

Serving English learners. An entire book could be written about how data can and should scaffold our work with nonnative English speakers. Why? Data tell us about a student's exposure and experience with the English language and provide an instructional starting point. That's the obvious use, but we can also use data to drill down into specifics that explain intricacies in a child's story we may never have known. Let's consider a few pertinent examples of ways to use data:

- *To provide insight when EL students are struggling academically.* No one has figured out a magic process or formula for supporting a student with limited English who may also have a learning disability. It's a messy, confusing, and emotional undertaking, further complicated by challenges in communicating with the parents along the way. What can help? Data, especially when they show a pattern of learning difficulties over time.

- *To create a thorough student learning profile and establish service delivery.* Most school-based assessments contain elements of reading and writing, but EL assessments also typically include speaking and listening components. Results, then, provide a more comprehensive snapshot of a student's ability to communicate effectively. When deciding how to provide service for a student, we need a complete profile; for example, a student might do well reading texts in English but may not be comfortable speaking or hearing it. What rich information data can provide in deciding how to support an English learner!

- *To support staffing decisions and resource allocation.* Because we use data to determine service needs, we also need data to communicate with departments of human resources or finance about staffing needs. If data are showing a sharp uptick in EL enrollments or a broad distribution of native languages, your school likely needs increased EL staff or bilingual aide support, and the shift certainly necessitates additional professional development, training, and resources. In our district, we used data to justify the purchase of a subscription-based translation service that gave us 24-hour telephone services for conversations with parents and students. It was a game-changer. Further, after implementing the service, we had even more data—how often we used the translation service, what times of day and times of year, which languages we accessed most, and how frequently we were communicating with parents.

- *To supplement parental reporting.* Another actionable use of data with EL students comes with an issue rarely discussed, but notably applicable, for any principal leading an EL program. When students are enrolled in a school district, we rely on parents to give us an accurate picture of a student's native language to make placement decisions. But how many times have we been tripped up on the inaccuracies of parent disclosure? Sometimes, parents will tell us the student is a native English speaker because somewhere along the way they heard that complete assimilation into an English environment is the fastest and most beneficial way to become a fluent speaker. Other times, they are part of a culture that eschews direct English instruction. Taking a parent's disclosure as fact, we may later find out that a student knows virtually no English and was set to receive no services, based on the parent's decision or misinformation. Still other times, parents misunderstand why enrollment forms ask about other languages spoken at home and will proclaim a bilingual expertise that doesn't really exist. Last year, we had a parent write on an enrollment form that Spanish was spoken in the home. The students were put through extensive EL testing, but the results were so confusing that we called the students' father for more information. He said, "I took four years of Spanish in high school," and he "wished" he had time to "speak it more" at home. He felt enrolling them as "bilingual" would make his children more "marketable" (for what, we weren't sure). The point, here, of course, is assessment and data will help us tease out what services are needed for a student, what phonological knowledge the student might have in English, and how we can structure a learning plan for a non-native speaker.

Planning and focusing classroom instruction. Gone are the days when all students were taught the same thing at the same time at the same pace. What *is* here to stay? Differentiated and personalized learning environments. For classrooms to flourish under these circumstances, wide-ranging data analysis must be part of the planning process, as it can supplement classroom assessment data and anecdotal evidence to help teachers plan and differentiate their instruction. The principal can guide expectations and provide support for teachers as they balance all factors—formative and summative assessments as well as information about student attentiveness, focus, and behaviors.

Supporting gifted learners. States vary on how students must be identified and served as gifted learners, and districts also interpret expectations differently. Dealing with this issue can be overwhelming for principals, especially because (keeping in mind that generalizations are never entirely accurate) parents of gifted students tend to be very active in seeking answers about their children's identification score, service plans, and academic progress. These conversations have the potential to get difficult, as emotions often take over and school staff can feel defensive and excessively questioned. The answer, then, is data. Many states and districts have a specific cut-off score that determines whether a child is identified as a gifted learner, and teachers can supplement that identification with formative data collected in the classroom over time. I've been part of many conversations about student giftedness; I rely on data (and state guidelines) to set the foundation for how we will serve a gifted child and then rely on teacher explanations of formative classroom data to make a specific plan for the student's instruction.

Planning for curricular updates and resource selection. Our district recently rewrote our K–12 health curriculum. It was up for review anyway, based on predetermined, board-adopted curriculum cycles, but we also had multiple data points nudging us to address concerns related to student mental health. We'd given surveys to students and parents that indicated many students were struggling with anxiety and low self-efficacy. We used the data to pinpoint exactly how and why we would incorporate direct instruction, guidance services, and ongoing assessment to measure student awareness of and growth related to these issues. Using data in this way (in any content area, really) helps keep subjectivity out of the equation, so decisions are made free of emotion and assumption.

Informing teacher feedback. When I evaluate teachers, I don't necessarily determine their effectiveness (or lack thereof) based on data from only one group of students, for all the reasons mentioned above. Instead, I give teachers feedback on their thoughtful and comprehensive use of various forms of data. "How do you plan your instruction with differentiation for individual students?" I'll ask. If a teacher tells me about one data point from a standardized test, I'll be glad that the teacher considered a solid, standardized source of information. If the teacher tells me about a student who had a low score on a computerized assessment *because* he tends to hurry through formal assessments *and* shows signs of testing anxiety, *but* consistently turns in excellent work *if* given a quiet space to work *and* frequent check-ins along the way, *and* has a particular gift in technology and prowess in public presentation, I'll be thrilled that the teacher truly knows her students and understands how to get the best from them. That's the kind of feedback that matters most.

Too Much Data?

We've just reviewed legitimate uses for data and reasons to love what data can do for us and our schools. But assessment and data can easily turn into a monster, making principals grow resentful and feel the value is trumped by the drawbacks. Here are a few reasons why data can make us quiver.

Overtesting in a quest for more and more data. Recently, one of my colleagues counted how many days his elementary school administered a district- or state-mandated test in a single month's time. Out of 22 school days, no fewer than 17 had at least one grade level taking some sort of test. This isn't true of every month, of course, but it did highlight a very real problem: with too much assessment, we lose the time to *teach.*

Forgetting that the measure highlights just one point in time. This drawback might be the biggest frustration for educators. High-stakes assessment data reflect just a single day—perhaps just one morning or afternoon—just one little blip in a lifetime of learning and growing. Relying too heavily on one score goes against what we know to be true: that to know our students well, whether they are 8 or 18, we need a whole lot of information. We need a series of data reports to truly understand them—if, in fact, we ever really can, especially when we think about all the growing and changing they have ahead of them.

Misconstrued results. Knowing that data cannot and do not thoroughly describe a student, it's especially frustrating when a data report is misread or generalized, leading to incorrect assumptions regarding the reasons behind a particular test score. A while ago in my state, we administered a particular test to much fanfare and worry, but there were so many problems with the format of the questions, the process for administration, and the results that the whole thing was scrapped after one year. State officials scrambled, the legislature rallied and voted quickly, and the next year we administered a different test. The experience highlighted the risk of misconstruing results, because missteps are likely to happen *even with the initial selection of an appropriate test.* To make wide-ranging generalities about students and their instruction based on a test we don't know much about—or whose longevity is uncertain—is hugely unsettling, especially if teachers, principals, schools, districts, even entire state education systems are evaluated or judged based on the results.

Public misunderstanding. Trying to get the public to grasp all the reasons, results, and repercussions of assessments and the ensuing data is a massive job. Our students' parents likely took one or two standardized tests in their entire school career, and those may have involved newsprint booklets and filling in answer bubbles with #2 pencils. After the tests were completed, no one ever heard much about the results. Fast-forward to today's world, where *data* and *assessment* are as common in educators' vocabulary as *summative* and *formative;* but to our public, these are all buzzwords covering a complicated and impenetrable world. To try to bridge public distance and confusion with real, accurate knowledge feels like an impossible task and, I would argue, contributes to many a principal's frazzledness and fatigue. Added to this sense of impossibility are states' attempts to explain assessments and data to the public through report cards or graphic-based generalized summaries. For a principal, trying to explain stanines, percentiles, RIT scores, growth projections, value added, and even the difference between ability and achievement is a never-ending task.

So what is a principal to do? I've found success by sticking to four strategies:

1. *Fill up teachers' toolboxes.* Teachers need to serve as the principal's microphone and messenger. If teachers have a solid

understanding of the terms, rationale, and longitudinal scope of data, they can communicate it in ongoing and consistent conversations with parents.

2. *Don't make a data report more than it is.* Because I know data represent just one point in time, that's precisely how I use data reports. "On this particular day, your child showed us that he is in the *xx*th percentile. What we've seen in the classroom throughout this year indicates . . . ." I always frame data conversations with the caveat that the data provide one piece of information. When I do that, the message I send is this: Is this valuable information? Sure. Is it the best and only information? Absolutely not.

3. *Look for other ways to collect data and use the information in immediate, more applicable ways.* Find data elsewhere and make the information part of any and all conversations about students and their journey of learning. This suggestion is intended not to diminish traditional data sources but to balance out those sources. In fact, that is what we'll do next in this chapter: consider specific ways to expand our collection of and response to data.

4. *Don't spend money on a program or vendor that promises better test results.* Rather, invest in what it takes to improve and strengthen good teaching.

Using Data in Alternative Ways

Many of us focus only on data from state and local standardized tests. How might we step out of the confines of that custom? How might we start gathering—and responding to—data that provide us with more immediately applicable information on patterns and trends? Here are some ideas to find and use data in unconventional but useful ways.

Athletics

How are our athletes handling the balance of academics and athletics? Are students on some athletic teams more successful in the classroom than those on other teams? If so, what are those coaches doing that might be replicated across an entire athletic department? A colleague of mine told me that academic progress on his school's baseball team was consistently lackluster and unpredictable. Players seemed to scorn the whole process of learning, thinking their place on the baseball team somehow trumped their responsibilities as students. Meanwhile, players on the lacrosse team consistently saw a rise in their grades and achievement while they were in season. My colleague pulled the data and studied trends, and he saw that the trend held true over multiple years. With factual data to support him, he was able to share the information with his athletic director and make a specific plan for developing coaches with an eye toward a consistent expectation (and accompanying strategies) for all teams.

Extracurricular Activities

Extracurricular activities face the same challenges, scrutiny, and pressures as many athletic teams, so the things we learn by studying trends in the athletic department can be applied to other departments, too. Do students in theater, student government, music, and related arts perform consistently in the classroom? Are there obvious patterns that can be traced to the expectations and support of the advisor? Are the incentives for students different in some way? What are the implications for the rest of the school? Data can help formulate and address questions that affect students outside—and therefore inside—the classroom.

Staff Attendance

Many principals lose sleep over poor staff attendance. The issue doesn't involve all staff; it's usually a small percentage who do the "call off all Fridays" thing. Studying teacher absenteeism over time, and correlating it with data on student growth and achievement, can be a starting point for change-evoking conversations with chronically absent staff about repercussions of their absenteeism.

Discipline

I find it fascinating to study data related to discipline. There are all sorts of ways to study the topic—by number of behavior referrals in a given time period, for example, but also by location, time of day, gender, race, and so on. I have a principal colleague who tracked how much time students spent in the office or removed from school owing to discipline issues, and then aligned it to academic achievement data. The results were enlightening and led to a few eye-opening conversations with staff about their biases and the implications of office referrals on academic growth.

Referral breakdowns by teacher. One of my favorite analyses is the breakdown of behavior referrals by teacher. Some teachers have a gift for handling tricky classroom behaviors, whereas others seem to seek out (and even escalate) discipline problems. I've had teachers who never, ever send a student to the office—or if they do, it's for an egregious offense that can't be ignored. I have other teachers who seem to send students to the office without a second thought, eager to shift the responsibility and problem to someone else. It's instructive to pull discipline data by teacher and really scrutinize the information. Many times, it validates the things I notice (and teachers' reputations) with hard data. It also helps me with certain decisions I have to make, including the following:

- *Guiding the response to a referral.* If a teacher who never reports an incident of student misbehavior actually *does* report one, it's a sign that the issue needs my immediate attention. I never dismiss a referral from a teacher who is a proven behavior expert; conversely, if I get a referral from a teacher who sends students to the office for every little thing, I approach it with dual purpose: to figure out if the student's behavior was really worth a referral and to try to support the teacher in finding new ways to manage the classroom.

- *Class placement.* Teachers with low numbers of discipline referrals tend to have stronger skills in developing relationships with students. When building a master schedule and placing particular students in classes or with teachers, it's nice to know that a certain teacher may have a higher likelihood of student success in the classroom and to know which teachers to avoid. This isn't to say that the strongest teachers should always have the most challenging students. Not at all.

We all know how unfair that can be, and how it can lead to fatigue in our best teachers. Every now and then, though, we can use data to determine what student profile cannot and should not be placed in a particular classroom.

Finding alternative solutions. A few years ago, we were ready to pull out our hair after repeated referrals of a 5th grade girl who continually got into fights at recess. They weren't small fights, either; the student would effectively haul off and punch anyone who irritated her in any way. The assistant principal had tried every tool and trick we could think of: mentoring, guidance, behavior plans, parental involvement, incentives, tough love, suspensions, and everything in between. Nothing worked; with every intervention, the student would sit in stony, silent fury, with narrowed eyes and crossed arms. Finally, we pulled the data. "Look at this," I said. "Every single incident this year has happened at recess." It was shocking we hadn't thought of it earlier, but having the information in front of us made it glaringly obvious—which is the gift and beauty of data. "We need to remove this 30-minute hotspot out of her day," we agreed. A former teacher of the student, well known for her outreach and supportive work with struggling students, offered to host the student in her classroom to serve as a reading buddy to younger students. Just like that, our problem was solved. The student loved her "job," the younger students benefited, the teacher felt like she was doing a really good thing to help out in a meaningful way, and other classmates were no longer subject to the student's difficulties at recess. In time, the student was able to articulate the triggers behind her recess troubles, confiding in her former teacher that the unstructured, frenzied pace of recess made her feel emotionally and physically anxious, which manifested itself in anger and physical outrage. She was, and would continue to be, a child who succeeded with smaller groups and in a calm atmosphere. Data helped us identify the antecedent to her behaviors, and our simple solution gave her the time and environment to learn how to articulate when, why, and how she would struggle. It was the first step in teaching her how to successfully advocate for herself.

Bus discipline. I look at data from bus referrals frequently and use the information in collaboration with our transportation coordinator. Together, we make sure drivers and teachers communicate about students who struggle on the bus. The information gives the drivers and teachers common goals and a shared understanding about students. It can help us in unconventional ways, too. A few years ago, one particular driver's data indicated terrible discipline issues on the way to school but none on the way home. Almost all factors were unchanged: the same 40 students rode both ways, all lived in one massive apartment complex, and all boarded and disembarked at the same three bus stops. The only difference was the route taken. The driver took a shorter route with multiple stoplights on the way to school and took the highway on the way home, because the GPS indicated it would be faster. As an experiment, the driver started taking the highway both ways. To our surprise, all behavior problems virtually disappeared. We don't know exactly why (we assume the action and distraction of a constantly moving bus keeps the students forward-focused more than the stationary intervals at stoplights), but we know it works. Thanks to data, we found a solution and could verify its effectiveness.

Special Education

Data can help principals know whether their special education programs are effective and good decisions are being made. I'll never forget the day that one of my supervisors called and asked why so many of our students were receiving special education services. I felt attacked, as though we were being accused of overqualifying or overserving students, but I didn't have answers for him. I dug in and studied the data. It turned out that 75 percent of students who had qualified for special education that year had been moved into our school with an IEP already in place from a previous district. Of the remaining 25 percent who *had* qualified at our school, 100 percent had been through a thorough Response to Intervention process. I showed my supervisor the data. He responded with respect and admiration, not only for the way we were servicing students but also for having data to explain and justify our work.

I also use data to anchor conversations about special education staffing in my building. We have a large and transient student population, and our staffing needs change often and without warning. As an example, when we have a few high-needs students move to other schools, it would be easy for our human resources department to cut one or two paraprofessionals from our staffing allocation. Using data from multiple years, I can show that although our special education population may change from month to month, it remains remarkably consistent over the course of a school year or several years; so if they cut a paraprofessional in response to student transiency one month, it's highly likely they'll need to add the position back again the next month. Data allow me to advocate for a consistent staffing model in which we hold tight through the inevitable ebbs and flows of our population, relying on the same staff members throughout an entire school year.

Screen Time

Parents worry about how to control screen time at home, but I wonder sometimes if we ought to be thinking about how much screen time happens at school. As many schools have shifted to one-to-one technology, some students are spending massive amounts of time looking at a screen. It isn't difficult to track how much time students spend on school-issued computers. I plan to collect some of these data over several years and compare the results with other data—attendance, discipline, academic growth, completion of assignments, grades, and achievement—to see if screen time affects our overarching purpose.

Longitudinal Data

For school districts, developing a data collection process to track student achievement from kindergarten through secondary school is a massive undertaking. How powerful can it be, though, to track how many students receive early intervention in reading or math—and how it affects them later, in high school and beyond? What about tracking student progress and intervention in early grades, and studying connections to special education services?

Our district is just now getting to this point, after years of hard work, and it remains a challenge to get teachers to truly understand the value in seeing a student's academic history. It's also very difficult to catch data from students who have moved into the district, because records are generally spotty or difficult to decipher. This is the kind of thing data reports are great for, though, and we could all benefit from increasing our commitment to and comfort with the benefits of long-term data collection.

Staff Concerns

A teacher came to me in a fury. She was just venting, she said, but she was sick and tired of all the interruptions to her teaching. There were *way* too many people coming in and out of her room throughout each day. "I know we are lucky to have all this extensive support staff," she said, "but I have special education staff, EL teachers, and paraprofessionals in my room throughout the day, and various other teachers come in and out of the room to borrow materials, ask questions, and even just visit. I feel like I can never really hit my stride."

"I know you're 'just venting' to me," I said, "but you have a legitimate and concerning point." I asked her to gather some data over the next few weeks and come back to me. We were both gobsmacked to realize she had an average of 18 interruptions a day. I asked other teachers if they had similar data and found that most did. I moved swiftly, pointing out the problem to the staff and asking them to rethink how and why they might visit (interrupt) a classroom. Special education and EL teams adjusted their schedules to limit how many visits they made to a single classroom in the course of a day, and we had conversations about the professional respect we needed to offer one another during instructional time. The changes didn't eliminate interruptions, but that wasn't our goal; instead, we just wanted to be more mindful of the *when* and *why* behind them. This is just one example of how a principal might use data to address staff concerns. Rather than react with frustration, emotion, or maintaining the status quo, you can respond with "Show me the data that are driving your concern." Then you'll have solid information on which to base decisions.

A Few More Ideas

Figure 6.1 shows a few ideas for data collection topics and thought-provoking questions for your staff, students, and parents. There are no correct or incorrect answers to the questions, but they may spark some interesting and productive conversations, and may even lead to impressive improvement and change.

When It's OK to Pull Back from Data

I once worked with a teacher who was beloved by students, parents, and colleagues. Students spent years hoping they'd end up in his class, and every summer when teacher assignments came out, I could count on phone calls from dismayed parents whose children had not been assigned to his class, many demanding a meeting with me and insisting on a schedule change. And he really was that good; I had spent a lot of time in his classroom and knew it was an instructional environment with unique and real-life applicability. His standardized assessment data showed mediocre results. Did I care? No. The fact that I had parents crying in my office because they so desperately wanted their child to be taught by this man was enough for me. He made students love school and become inquisitive, eager learners. That was a pretty important "data point" for me, and I never let one standardized test divert me from acknowledging his gift as a teacher.

Let's conclude this chapter by considering a few times when it is perfectly permissible to take a step back from data and rethink the role data play in your decision making.

When data reports are all you're talking about. Students are far more than data. I shudder to think how I, as an adult, would be judged if I were grouped, graded, or defined only by a test I had just taken. How could it possibly capture everything that I am? How irresponsible, then, to be a leader who overemphasizes data by making the results of data gathering a focal point in all conversations. On the contrary, data should be just a fraction of what we consider—especially when we're talking about children, who haven't begun to finish becoming who they will grow up to be.

FIGURE 6.1

Data Collection Topics and Questions

Topic	Questions
Student engagement and wellness	• What is the attendance rate for students involved in extracurricular activities versus those who are not? • If your district provides flu shots for students, how many receive them? Of those who do, how many miss school because of flu-related symptoms?
Teacher engagement	• How many days does your district allocate to teachers for professional development? • How many in-house professional development opportunities are available in your school and district? • How much money is spent on outside professional development?
Organizational health	• Do the demographics, ethnicity, and cultural diversity of your teaching staff reflect your community? • What percentage of teachers are involved in a negotiating unit? What about classified staff? • What is the staff turnover rate? • What is the allocation of district funds for human resources versus facilities versus instructional materials?
Student engagement and connectedness	• How many field trips or school-related absences do students take per year? • How much time is spent on activities completely unrelated to the academic or social-emotional growth of students (e.g., fundraising, movies unrelated to curricular requirements)? • Is there a way to survey students to measure their thoughts about school? • What data are available about use of resources? For example, how many library books are checked out? How often is technology used? How often do students log on to online intervention programs?

When data make you defensive. For me, defensiveness pops up when I feel I am being held responsible for something I can't control. A close derivative is when I am surprised by something I should have seen but didn't. When analyzing school data reports, it is easy to immediately defend, explain, and excuse. But data shouldn't make us feel we are defendants on trial. Nor, incidentally, should we feel like plaintiffs or prosecutors. I like to shift the analogy and think of it as a football game. I can play defense, or I can play offense. On defense, I am reacting to what happens to me. On offense, though, I am fully in charge of my own efforts, practice, and planning, and I can calmly confront information in front of me. If we leave our defensiveness behind and insist on playing offense, we can ask questions about the information that might lead to real change and noticeable improvement: "What does this information reveal about our school? Are there actionable steps we can take to respond to it?" Blame isn't the point, so playing defense is unnecessary; on the contrary, taking an offensive stance can give data the role of teammate rather than adversary.

When pressured to do something that doesn't feel right. Principals have a constant mantra running through their minds: *Is this decision in the best interest of students?* This question is our true north and what we must remember as we swim in the shark-infested waters of data and assessment. If something comes along that doesn't feel right or doesn't seem to benefit kids, it's time to push the eject button and get back to our purpose. I experienced this when navigating a tricky situation with a student being considered for retention under the mandates of a state law. He did not "pass" multiple attempts at a standardized test, and the law was clear: data showed he had not reached a particular benchmark, so he would have to repeat a grade level. The thought of it made me feel ill. I knew retention would devastate him on all levels—socially, emotionally, and academically. This student had made multiple moves between multiple states, leading to huge gaps in his schooling, and he had behavior and anger issues that blocked his "typical" learning experience. His only crime, it seemed, was his family's decision to move to our state at that particular time in his educational journey. It would have been far easier for me to shrug my shoulders, point at the data, and tell his family he would be repeating the grade. Doing so didn't feel right, though, so I fought back and I fought hard. Using a couple of options and waivers and relying on data and special-education processes, we were ultimately able to promote him to the next grade with intervention supports in place.

When data are used to quiet you, shame you, or throw you off course. In your efforts to do the right thing for kids, you will inevitably encounter people who will ask hurtful, condescending questions, cloaked beneath data, to divert your attention away from your greater purpose. This happened to me several years ago when I was attending a data-review training session. My school's student population had more than 20 percent nonnative English speakers. We had high rates of socioeconomic disadvantage, and most of our students were from single-parent homes. Our students were progressing—our data clearly showed it—but not at a rate that would make headlines or win us a "Most Improved" trophy.

A woman sitting across from me, an assistant professor at a local university, asked, "What do you plan to do with these data?" I knew her to be someone who had never taught in a classroom or led a school, but she was a self-proclaimed "school change agent" and relied on data reports (concerning students she'd never met) as her prime decision-making factor.

"Nothing," I said. "Our students have bigger problems than how they perform on these tests."

"Are you saying learning to read isn't important?"

I wasn't saying that at all. I tried again to explain. "Learning to read is very important. More than that, though, I want our school to be a safe place for our students. I want them to be hard workers, kind to others, and feel they have value in our school and in this world. Their test scores aren't my highest priority."

"It sounds like you're deprioritizing their academic growth. Don't you believe all kids can learn? Even those—especially those—with disadvantages?"

Again, that's not what I was saying. In fact, I was saying the opposite, at a much deeper level.

I knew she was regurgitating questions she thought would be provocative and somehow helpful, but to me, they were judgmental and out of touch. I didn't try to explain myself. Yes, I believe all kids can learn. I just don't want standardized tests, which are universally agreed to be written in a way that puts some students at a disadvantage, to define who they are or, worse, who they will become.

● ● ●

When our love-hate relationship with the information we get from data collection oscillates toward hate, it's because its myriad interpretations and uses can so easily divert us from doing good, meaningful work with it. There's no reason we can't swing the pendulum back toward a commonsense approach, though, simply by broadening the lens we use to study the data. We can reframe data for use in various ways, for various purposes, toward a more meaningful, applicable outcome.

Revisit Operations: Reviewing Procedures and Resources to Reclaim Operational Excellence

It was a bad day. I was bogged down by too much to do and too little time to do it. My boss stopped by as part of her rotational school visits, and I was glad to see her. Nothing seemed to be going well, and I needed a supportive ear. She walked with me to a classroom where I'd been called to try to calm a student having a behavioral crisis. "Some days I'd like to just quit this job and go back to the classroom," I grumped. "It would be so nice. I'd just lock myself in my classroom, teach my heart out, and leave at 3 o'clock every day like some teachers do."

She laughed out loud. "You'd be in the poor principal's office every day with a better, faster, smarter way to do things."

"I wouldn't!" I protested.

"You would. If you had a principal who didn't specialize in efficiency and operational excellence, it would drive you bananas."

I had to concede. I love thinking about the best ways to be efficient and effective with our school operations, and I get uneasy when things are clunky, slow, or nonsensical. In fact, one of the things I love most about being a principal is recognizing when a decision needs to be made and knowing that I'm the one who can take the reins, weigh the options, think it through, and *decide*. I establish a plan, communicate with everyone involved, and watch the whole thing move along. It's worth noting here that "efficient" doesn't necessarily mean "fast." There are times when the decision making is done in a minute or two; other times, it takes months. But I get energy from being the leader who gets to determine how it all plays out. I've grown to love overseeing a seamless, efficient process. I love it to a fault, perhaps, because there is a pretty big downside: I get fraught when stalled by inefficiency in the areas I can't control.

Several years of unprecedented growth in my district put my school in the crosshairs of two challenging issues: unexpected enrollment spikes and outdated attendance and residency zones. District leadership held several meetings to brainstorm solutions for the upcoming school year, and I was pleased to be invited. We all knew any solution was just a temporary bandage to cover the bleeding until voter-approved building construction caught up with our needs. I went into the meetings with swagger. I felt confident I knew how to fix our problem and was certain about what wouldn't work—or at least what would be more trouble than it was worth. I had several bosses who thought differently.

The meetings didn't go well from the start. I was too verbal, too aggressive, too smarty-pants. I found myself in a bit of hot water, asked (in the most professional way) to shush. It was a new feeling for me, and I didn't like it at all.

But in the end, I was just the principal. Our directors of operations, student safety, and transportation had more knowledge and perspective. They also had more power and clout. They were right to move in a direction they felt was best, even though it went against my wishes and recommendations. The experience felt like a loss, though, and I had to marinate in it for a while, seeking a way to keep my attitude positive and team-oriented. I understood all the reasons my solutions were not selected, but it took conscious emotional labor to recognize the real issue: as a principal, there are things I can control and things I unreservedly cannot. Complicating matters, too, is that the rules aren't always the same; they change with the situation and they change with the district leadership.

The experience was a valuable lesson for me, as it is for all of us principals. Sure, we are in charge of the operations of our buildings, but only up to a point. District leaders have the ultimate decision-making power, as well they should; they are paid to oversee the operations of the entire system and make the best decisions using a lens wider than the one we hold at the building level.

Wise principals constantly adjust, assimilate, and alter how they approach operational decisions, depending on the situation. If I could walk away from this chapter with one goal achieved, it would be for principals to identify when they can—and should—take control and, when they do, to have the confidence to advocate professionally and fiercely for efficiency in school operations.

No one else can take on this responsibility as well as we can; no one else knows our building's needs like we do. Further, if we don't continue advocating and working toward operational excellence, we may feel helpless, disillusioned, and—yes—very weary. There *are* many facets of our jobs over which we have no control. We *are* often hamstrung by inefficiency, bad decision making, archaic practices, and ridiculous, repetitive, ineffective systems. These things can be a primary factor in why principals experience burnout. To be held accountable for a school's operations but to have little voice in the matter is demoralizing and dispiriting.

In this chapter, we'll open by discussing why excellence in operations matters so much. We'll talk about your sphere of influence—when to push for change and when to raise your hands in surrender. And we'll talk about specific areas in which you can revitalize and improve a school's efficiency and productivity.

Efficiency and Excellence in Operations: Why It Matters

If you've never worked in a system that is bogged down with inefficient, archaic operations and technology snafus, you're lucky.

Inefficiency and outdated systems are common in all kinds of educational settings—most often in huge districts. When there are tens of thousands of students and teachers to contend with, making changes or updating practices can feel like trying to move a ship in a creek: slow, impossible, and painfully unlikely to succeed. That's not to say this is easy in smaller districts; school leaders and principals in small communities must navigate the change process while juggling many other responsibilities, all without the support of an administrative team or central office staff.

Here's the bottom line: if we are spending time addressing the repercussions of inefficient operations, then we're not doing things we *should* be doing. We can't be instructional leaders or innovative trailblazers when we are buried beneath paperwork and dealing with information management, broken equipment, staff management, and facility problems. I've handled all sorts of challenges and don't mind doing so *unless* the root cause can be traced back to fragmented operational systems.

For a long time, our human resources department had a rule that every open position required three full interviews and, upon selection of a potential hiree, a four-part reference check. I appreciated these standards, with one exception: crossing guards. With hundreds of students crossing dangerous intersections on their way to and from school, our district hires crossing guards, knowing student safety is worth the financial investment. But finding people for the position was difficult, given the dismal pay, unappealing hours, often miserable weather, and unpleasant task of stopping harried commuters. I knew, because I'd had to step in as a crossing guard whenever we had an unfilled spot. I was thrilled if I had someone who actually *wanted* the job.

Not many did. Most often, when we posted a position, applicants were simply looking to "get in" the district—to get hired and then, as soon as possible, apply for another job as a secretary, a paraprofessional, or another supporting role. Our union contract required that current employees receive first crack at open positions, so it was well known that getting a job as a crossing guard was a good way to get a *different* job. As a result, applicants were usually overqualified but would take the position and quit as soon as they got a shot at something better. Occasionally I found a candidate who actually *did* want to be a crossing guard, but the person would quickly find it to be wretched work and, like the others, quit.

Having been burned too many times, I decided to take a different approach when I had an unexpected crossing guard opening: I recruited. I approached a parent I knew well. She was kind, smart, and dependable. She walked her four kids to and from school every day. I asked her, "Would you want to make 20 bucks every time you do this?"

"Sure," she said, happy for the opportunity.

That's when I ran into trouble with HR. They insisted I had to interview three candidates, and if we didn't have three applicants, we'd have to wait until we did. I protested vehemently, but they were adamant: "Sorry. Policy."

Doing my best to conceal my irritation, I asked if I could take some time to collect my thoughts and resume our conversation in a couple of days. I took lot of deep breaths while crafting a rebuttal based on common sense, efficient use of time and resources, and input and support from other principals in our district, all of whom felt as I did about the issue. In the end, our HR director relented and the policy was changed to give principals a little more latitude in hiring for difficult-to-fill positions.

To be clear, I understood why HR had implemented this hiring rule. It was a good one; it just needed an exception. Getting that exception gave me some control over what had been an uncontrollable situation and ended up saving hours of time—time that I could spend on other, more important aspects of my job as principal.

A Shifting Sphere of Influence

If all principals lined up to describe our operational challenges, we would have thousands of completely different answers. Even if we just start with facilities, the responses would be far-ranging. Some of us spend our days in buildings that are literally cracking at the seams; others are in buildings so new they still smell like fresh flooring. Some of us look out our office windows at cornfields, others at high-rises; others don't have a window—or an office. In most cases, there is little we can do to improve or change our facilities. It's a sad and frustrating truth.

I once visited a small rural school in which the facilities were horrifying. It had been years since anything had been painted, decades since anything had been remodeled or fixed. Water fountains were inoperable; furniture was cracked and abandoned in hallways; mouse droppings and water stains decorated the floor. The day I was there, one of the buses broke down and there was no working replacement, so the route simply wasn't completed. Some kids got rides to school; others just didn't come that day. It made me want to weep—not necessarily at the awfulness of the facility (though that was, indeed, heartbreaking) but because I'd just been to a school 20 miles east that gleamed and glittered in newness. Going there was like going to Oz.

What was the difference?

Well, nothing, in terms of location and student need—but everything, too. The schools were part of a state education system with a complicated school funding method that, some years back, had relied on school superintendents to accept state financial support based on certain conditions (including matching district funds provided by community votes on a levy/bond issue). Some superintendents had jumped on the deal; others couldn't or wouldn't. Some communities voted for a tax increase to provide necessary matching funds; others didn't. It was a maddening and inequitable system, and now, years later, students were the ones paying the price.

For years, it has been virtually impossible for principals to influence such laws, standards, and scenarios. But recently, and increasingly, educators have taken on an advocacy role, and some are pursuing political office. This development gives me hope. The shift is a slow one, though, and until it begins to make a noticeable difference, the only real option principals have is to accept what we cannot change and find energy in what we can.

Usually we find that energy by lifting up and empowering teachers, supporting parents, and helping students have the best school experience possible. One way we can accomplish those things is by taking on the challenges that lead to operational excellence. A good place to start is eliminating outdated practices.

Eliminating Outdated Practices

Those of us who have been principals for some time have clear memories of how things used to be. Teachers would call the principal early in the morning, on an actual telephone, to report that they were sick. Office staff communicated with notes slipped into our mailboxes. Attendance was taken on slips of paper that were hung on a clip outside our classroom doors and gathered up by a secretary or student helper. Student schedules were printed on dot-matrix printers, and when changes were needed, a seven-step information process kicked in, with phone calls and checklists and all sorts of opportunities for errors. Now all these things can be done with a couple of keystrokes.

Identifying specific opportunities to eliminate outdated practices depends on so many factors that it is best addressed at the individual school level. For principals, change begins by asking, of self and staff, "Is there something we don't need to be doing anymore? Any way to do it better?" Often schools just stick with what has worked, never stopping to question if there is a better way.

In many districts, the handling of management tasks ranks high on the list of outdated practices. That need not be the case. We are lucky to be school leaders at a time when online management systems are available. Many management tasks used to require extensive time and human capital, mostly to complete paperwork, file records, and push information around. Now it can all be handled with massive data dumps and regular software updates.

In our district, we have online management systems in place for all sorts of things: student scheduling; academic progress monitoring; special education; attendance tracking; student lunch orders, accounts, and free/reduced-price lunch management; facility management and maintenance; technology work tickets; student discipline; and student health records. None of these systems is perfect,

I suppose, but they're all immeasurably better than our old ways of doing things.

For any principal bogged down with management of information, paperwork, or systems, it's a fruitful and fulfilling challenge to search out online management systems that can do this work for you or your staff. Vet as many vendors as you need to, but when you find a good system (preferably with strong customer support) and implement it, you'll wonder how you ever lived without it.

Three years ago, I challenged myself to go through my filing cabinet and get rid of every single folder. We had online information systems to handle everything in the cabinet, and if we didn't, I intended to develop one that would work for me. It took a while, but I was successful. I don't have a single manila folder in my office, leaving my workspace clean, clear, and uncluttered. I can find every piece of information I need on my computer or online. I am so grateful I don't have to go back to a time when we were using triplicate forms or searching for the right file folder.

Overseeing Technology

Most principals I know quake at the thought of overseeing technology: managing allocation, keeping track of usage, dealing with repairs, and supervising efficient use. Typically, technology is out of our comfort and knowledge zones. Not surprisingly, as is the case with most operational challenges, the role principals play in technology usage varies widely. For some, technology use is handled by a district department, so involvement is limited; in other cases, principals are the primary people responsible. Moreover, equity of resources varies considerably among and within schools. Some settings are fully one-on-one in terms of technology devices per student—a boon for principals committed to blended learning opportunities but an endless headache of related management issues. Others are thrilled to have a cart of laptops to share between departments and grade levels.

Because of our role as instructional leaders, the hope and goal would be that we aren't managing technology use and allocation single-handedly but have specific staff members to handle this important work for and with us. If not, I might suggest empowering teachers to take over this role (for a stipend, perhaps, if funds are available) to free up time to do important leadership work. In this case, the best solution to a problem may be careful, deliberate delegation.

School Safety and Security

Recently, school leaders have been allocating more energy and attention to safety and security. We've all gotten smarter, more careful, more aware, and certainly more focused on the safety and security of every single child in our building.

With that said, I actually take issue with the implication that we need to make schools more "safe." The vast majority of schools *are* safe—extremely safe. An *Education Week* article titled "Data: Schools Have Gotten Safer over Time" (Blad, 2018) points out that student victimization has actually decreased since 1992. When we hear people say, "Schools need to be safer," I presume what they *really* mean is they want schools to be immune from the risks and vulnerabilities present elsewhere in the world.

I recently led a full day of professional development on school safety. For eight exhausting hours, the staff discussed all components of school safety. We reviewed fire, tornado, evacuation, lockdown, and shelter-in-place procedures. We simulated scenarios. We did extensive preemptive planning and preparation for issues ranging from student mental health crises to intruders or active shooters.

At the beginning of the day, I created an online collaborative document to collect specific suggestions, ideas, and fears from teachers. "If something occurs to you that we haven't covered—anything you feel we could do to be more safe and secure—just make note of it," I told them.

I made the mistake of checking the document before leaving for the day. I was drained, sagging beneath the weighty implications of the issues we'd discussed. I should have waited to open the document, because when I did, I felt like I'd been kicked in the gut. It was a full 19 pages of suggestions. Though some were helpful and on point, the majority seemed extreme. Some "suggestions" were simply impossible or appeared to be based on a paranoia I believe is unhealthy in schools. "All our windows should be tinted, locked, and sealed," one person wrote. "Someone could hide in the bush outside one of our doors and slip in," wrote another. "Do we have a system for someone to check restrooms every few minutes for someone hiding there?"

I felt the staff wanted 20-foot concrete walls, armed officers around every corner, and bubble wrap around all of us. I closed my laptop and stepped away for a few days.

In the meantime, I consulted a few experts, sharing the staff responses with our school resource officer, several colleagues, and our director of student operations. They empathized with my sense of helplessness and vexation; they, too, were not sure how to satisfy all these requests and remarks. Asking for input had been wise, but I felt that much of the input given just wasn't practical enough or response-able.

But I'd asked for—and received—staff feedback, and now I needed to do something with it. I couldn't ignore it. School safety is such a hot topic, I knew I'd be misunderstood if I gave a response that seemed callous or dismissive. If I were to stand in front of my staff and say, "C'mon, guys, let's be reasonable here," I would be criticized, justifiably, for discounting their concerns as silly. An important thread of trust would be broken.

So, with help and time, I was able to recalibrate my response in the shared document. I added a new column to the chart, "Principal Response," in which I acknowledged each individual concern, offered suggestions for a solution, and welcomed help from staff in expanding the solutions. I responded to even the most outlandish comments. Then I shared the document with staff again, inviting further feedback in a final column titled "Additional Teacher Response."

Not a single staff member took the issue one step further. Not one word was added to the column for additional responses. In follow-up conversations, I found teachers were satisfied with our safety procedures and plans; I couldn't find a single indicator that there was truly anything further we could or should do. Here's what I learned from that experience.

Sometimes the best action is listening. Staff didn't really expect sweeping changes to our already robust safety procedures. They just appreciated having a place to document their latent worries and needed to know I heard them.

Use common sense. I've been admonished for saying this aloud, but there is no way we can make schools 100 percent immune from danger, just like we can't make airports, theaters, clubs, and concert venues completely safe. We absolutely *can* make our best effort, however. We can plan for the worst, and we can be ready to take on whatever comes our way. Common sense is our best friend in managing this insatiable need for an airtight, perfect plan, because there will always be a scenario we hadn't considered.

Weigh risk and reward. With common sense in our toolbox, we can weigh any action against the reaction. This point is essential when creating school safety procedures. Why? Because an unspoken contradiction surrounds the issue: we lock all the doors during the day and stop visitors to ask for identification, but then we open the doors and allow admission to everyone and anyone for a football game, performance, or holiday celebration. There is peace in the middle ground, though, if we evaluate the impact of all our decisions by asking, "Would a reaction be worse than the action?" If we put safety mandates in place based on a fraction of a percentage of likelihood (the action), we have to weigh if the reaction (limitations and diminishment of school and community experiences) is worth it. For example, if we determine recess is too dangerous and cancel it based on the low likelihood of an intruder on the playground, would the effect on student health and well-being be worth taking away this indisputably valuable break in a child's day?

Safety issues, conversations, and worries make everyone feel awful. Just thinking about the "what ifs" leaves a terrible feeling in the air. That doesn't mean we should bury it. But it helps to know it's a universal feeling. The best—and only—thing we can do is commit to using our resources in intelligent and reasonable ways and, at any given time, be confident that we are doing our best.

Safety is an all-the-time thing. When I first started teaching, the only time we thought about safety was during isolated fire and tornado drills. Times have changed. Safety is now something that is on our minds, and the minds of our staff and parents, pretty much all the time. Drills are no longer just once-a-month inconveniences; they are one piece in a larger plan. The mindset has shifted. I think of safety like a sieve; nothing of any essence can get through the filter of safety.

Transportation

Your district probably has a department that handles all transportation issues. These departments tend to be highly efficient. They have to be, because financial requirements and limitations insist that buses start up on time and cover large geographical areas with minimal cost and limited human resources. Most transportation directors have magnificent software to help make busing a seamless operation. In addition, add-on resources such as bus cameras help drivers improve student behaviors and respond to in-bus challenges.

It's when the buses pull up to our individual schools that many of us may benefit from studying our operational efficiencies. Here are a few questions to think about as you consider whether to take on a transportation issue at your school:

- How long does it take to load and unload buses? Is there a better, faster, safer way buses could line up, release students, and load students at the end of the day?
- Do your arrival and dismissal procedures allow for safe and efficient space for all transportation factors (buses, cars driven by parents, student drivers, walkers, cyclists)?
- Is there a system in place to quickly identify and solve problems, such as a student missing a bus?
- Are your bus policies and procedures reasonable and applicable?
- What is your role in safety drills and planning?
- Are drivers well trained in handling behavioral challenges that happen on the bus? If not, would the drivers appreciate your preemptive support?

- Are there modifications within your control that would improve efficiency (e.g., signage, traffic flow, use of staff for supervision)?

As a side note, I have always made it my business to build and maintain a strong relationship with bus drivers. I like and respect them, and I want them to feel the same about me. Sometimes the best tactic I have in my toolbox is expanding my collegial circle to include the people whose work directly affects mine.

Discipline Referral Systems and Management

I once interviewed a candidate for a job as an assistant principal who seemed almost desperate to get the job. At the time of his interview, he was serving as a principal in a neighboring district, so I was surprised at his zealousness; to me, it appeared that this job would be a step down. When I asked, I appreciated his honest answer. In his current role, he had no assistant principal or guidance counselor, so "all I do is discipline, all day long." He described a typical day in which he had done no more than greet all the students and settle in before a lineup started to form in the office. He investigated issues, decided on and distributed consequences, called parents, intervened, mediated, and filled out discipline paperwork—all day long, every single day. He'd tried implementing systems of positive behavior support; he'd provided professional development for his teachers; he'd consulted behavior specialists, read books, attended webinars, and sought ideas from colleagues. Nothing seemed effective.

No wonder he was exhausted. Of all the things that deflate a principal's energy and enthusiasm, a constant stream of discipline referrals might be the most destructive—and the most disheartening. When discipline issues pop up, everything you'd planned for the day comes to a screeching halt. If the problem is a significant one, requiring witnesses and statements and multiple calls or meetings with parents, it could well be days before there is resolution. This situation can't be seen, in anyone's imagination, as fun. And over time, it relentlessly chips away at our enthusiasm and spirit. Based on my experiences over the years, here are a few ideas to help prevent you from being buried under discipline issues.

Provide continual differentiated PD with teachers. Although all-staff professional development on discipline can be helpful in the right context and with the right delivery, it really doesn't help the teachers who have already mastered discipline management. I would much rather work with teachers individually. That way I don't insult the master teachers with training they don't need; I am simply differentiating my training for the situations and staff who need it. So when I notice a trend in which a teacher seems to be sending too many discipline referrals for insignificant issues without trying classroom interventions first, I'll request a meeting to review what I've noticed and provide ideas and support. A one-on-one meeting with the principal to discuss individual behavior challenges is significantly more effective than a generalized approach to professional development. This individualization requires an investment of time, certainly, but it's a lot better than time spent poring over the student handbook and talking on the phone, delivering bad news to parents.

Invest in the concept of "teacher power" versus "principal power." When a student is sent to the office for an offense that should have been managed by the teacher, it sends a message to all students that the teacher is powerless. It simultaneously puts the principal in the unwinnable position of investigating and overseeing a consequence, which practically begs for criticism (from student, parents, and teacher). And the consequences are rarely, if ever, effective. The discipline that school officials have to use is a lot like the prison system—everyone knows it doesn't work, but it's the only tool we have. What a shame. In truth, the only real power principals have is to be the final "heavy," and in the end, nothing new or helpful is truly accomplished.

Teachers, though? Teachers have power. They can work toward a relationship with the student, invest heavily in the student's success, connect with the family, prioritize social-emotional learning over academic learning, and devote time to peer systems that directly reward and incentivize all students or individual students.

Principals can't do any of that—not in a deep way, at least, and certainly not on a large scale. That's why principals should make it a mission to help teachers understand that they are the ones with the real power to make a difference in student behaviors. Again, it takes an investment of time—training, conversation loops, feedback cycles—but it is well worth it.

Distinguish between "discipline" issues and "guidance" issues. This distinction is a gray area, but it's worth consideration if you have a strong guidance counselor or guidance department. I used to oversee every discipline issue that was sent to me. I thought it was my job. Over time, I've learned that the guidance counselor can sometimes handle an issue more effectively than I can, especially when it involves conflict between students. If mediation and monitoring can fix a problem, why wouldn't I step back and let a master handle it? My counselor enjoys partnering with me on these sorts of things because he, too, would prefer to work toward a solution for students rather than have them be given consequences.

Consider class placement. Of course, this idea is more feasible in smaller schools, but careful individual placement of students in classrooms with teachers who excel in classroom and behavior management can be the best intervention available. We addressed this matter in Chapter 6, encouraging the use of data to place students, and it applies here as well; to limit discipline referral overload, your teachers are your best defense.

Leave a paper trail. I rely heavily on an online behavior management system to handle the entire discipline process. Teachers fill out a brief informational report before sending a student to the office. It provides the student's name, location of the incident, details of the infraction or allegation (with a distinction among what the teacher saw, what the teacher heard, what was reported to the teacher, and what the teacher suspects), and the names of any student or adult witnesses. Before I speak to the student, I read the referrals. During and after my investigation, I update the report with additional details, consequences, and a communication plan for parents. With a couple of clicks, the finalized report can be sent to every teacher with whom the student has contact. I can also generate documentation or necessary paperwork from this system, including Intent to Suspend forms, suspension forms, and any other document that needs to be signed and filed. This system reports directly to the state, fulfilling our requirement to report discipline infractions, trends, and volume for the state's information and reporting mandates. I've mastered this online system, so I move quickly and efficiently through these steps. The system has been a game-changer for me, and any principal could benefit from adjusting and auditing the way documentation and paperwork are managed in relation to discipline. Being buried under paperwork just makes an already challenging task feel unmanageable.

Staff Allocation, Schedules, and Responsibilities

I've been at my current school for five years. When I arrived, a master schedule had been in place for over a decade. The teachers liked it, and at first glance, there seemed to be no problems.

Well, *of course* the teachers liked the schedule, I discovered. They had a bus or supervisory duty just one week out of three. In other schools where I'd worked, teachers had a *daily* duty. At first, I didn't dare question the schedule because I didn't want to upend their equilibrium. I was also well aware that one of the teachers had created the schedule, and she was the one who updated it every year. She was masterful at scheduling, able to naturally divide the day into allocations of equal time and think about how "prep period" minutes and duty minutes could combine; she was well liked and respected, and everyone seemed to trust how things were. Let sleeping dogs lie, I thought.

As time passed, I began to grow uncomfortable. Our school had changed dramatically since the master template of the schedule was written. We had 200 more enrolled students, which meant significantly less space in common areas, hallways, and eating and study areas. We had also evolved to a more complex student demographic. With these changes and no corresponding changes to the master schedule, I was becoming convinced that the schedule didn't allocate enough teacher supervision. I didn't feel students were safe.

Another thing I noted was that our teachers had a long-standing tradition of swapping substitutes around to cover duties. If one teacher on the team was absent, the substitute plans would be altered to cover duties for anyone else on the team. Pretty soon, I noticed that many times there were *only* substitutes on duty. On days with a high number of teacher absences, it was quite possible that no "known" staff would be available during bus, lunch, and unstructured transitions.

This situation was a cultural conundrum as much as anything else. Long-standing operational traditions become embedded in a school's culture, and though they may have negative consequences, there was a risk that negating them would lead to a groundswell of teacher dissatisfaction. Again, the question arose: which is worse—the action or the reaction? I had to weigh whether to disband the tradition and risk discontent, or let it continue and risk student safety.

Using sticky notes, I started plotting a new staff schedule, frequently erasing my jottings. I did it quietly and on my own, taking lots of mental notes about things I noticed: what was working, what wasn't, and how I could manipulate minutes or staff schedules to improve it all. I spent spring break in my quiet, empty office creating a new, workable draft. When I felt I had a solid, well-planned rationale I could easily articulate, I brought the new plan to a meeting of our teacher leadership team.

This was the part I'd dreaded most, and it turned out to be the easiest. I explained my rationale, and to my surprise and relief, every teacher on the committee agreed with me, albeit grudgingly. Many had also felt uncomfortable with the schedule and mirrored my reasons, primarily related to unstructured transition times—too many kids, not enough staff available for supervision. They were 100 percent supportive of an increase in duties and promised to message our new direction to the teachers on their teams. They did give some suggestions for improving my draft, which I gladly incorporated. We presented the new draft to the whole staff, with leadership team members joining me to share the rationale. More input led to another draft, and then another. We had a final version in place by the start of the next school year, and we opened the year with a significantly beefed-up teacher presence during transitions and unstructured times. I slept well at night, knowing we were using staff efficiently and responsibly and, best of all, our students were well cared for.

Many of us let our schools fall into a rut in which the same staff members are responsible for the same duties every year, teaching and working in their own little bubbles. That can be a good thing if stability and consistency are the goal, but it can also lead to apathy and complacency. Here are a few things to consider if you are seeking the motivation to mix it up and improve how you use and allocate your human capital:

- Are current scheduling and procedures the best they can be for students?
- Are there staff members who could benefit from some sort of schedule change?
- Are there staff members who aren't pulling their weight? Staff members working too hard?
- Has your school changed in such a way that the "old ways" aren't working anymore?
- How have your school's demographics or student needs shifted over time, and has the school evolved with the change?
- Are there any safety issues with your current staffing and operational setup that concern you?
- Have you avoided updating or improving staff responsibilities for any particular reason?

● ● ●

When I reflect on any time I've made a change to improve operations, processes, or staff allocation, schedules, and responsibilities,

I am struck by how daunting the undertaking felt at the beginning. But the effort usually results in positive changes for our school and, perhaps more important, is part of a process that makes me a more empowered, more inspired, more informed principal. As with any new challenge successfully addressed, the payoff extends well beyond the initial outcome. Principals can resuscitate their energy, impact, and career longevity in countless ways by improving operational procedures.

8

Relax, Rediscover, Revive: Bringing Joy Back to the Principalship

When I speak to groups of principals, someone inevitably asks how I find balance between work and life. I answer honestly: *There is no balance.* There is, instead, a teeter-totter—a constant movement of up and down, up and down. Rather than feel seasick or unbalanced, we can make the conscious choice to enjoy the ride—embrace the ups, muscle through the downs, and remember that the work can be really fun, especially because it involves supporting young people. This chapter will offer reminders of why we went into this work in the first place and ideas for how to deliberately insert the joy back into our daily routines.

First, Go Back

Let's start by going back—way back. When I talk with principals who feel defeated, burned out, or frustrated, I ask them, "Can you remember why you wanted to be a principal in the first place?" Typically their answers fall into three themes: a desire to do more, a craving for change, and an instinct for leadership.

A desire to do more. Most principals started off as classroom teachers. Though teaching is an exhausting job and, when done well, is a noble and admirable life's work, for some people it can grow disheartening over time. I adored teaching English—until I didn't. I remember a moment when I thought I could not read one more student essay with missing capital letters or one more 500-word run-on sentence. I wanted to do *more*. So, although I fondly remember my days in the classroom, there came a time when I was decidedly ready to leave. I wanted to be stretched and challenged, and I wanted to feel I'd made a big difference in a new way.

Many of us moved into the principal role for a similar reason, yet we struggle to articulate it without sounding pretentious or condescending to the people we admire most—teachers. We don't want to be insulting when we say, "Teaching wasn't enough." But it wasn't.

A craving for change. Many leaders thrive on change. We like living in a state of professional curiosity: *What else is there for me to learn? How might I learn it?* This state of mind isn't necessarily a longing to go "higher," though sometimes that does happen—from teacher to principal to director to assistant superintendent to superintendent—but is instead rooted in an insatiable hunger to change things up on a regular basis. In the role of principal, change comes naturally through the rhythms of a school year, the spike and ebb of seasonal commitments, and the continual encountering of unexpected, idiosyncratic challenges.

An instinct for leadership. Over time, I've grown more certain that successful school principals can't be made; they are born. They have natural leadership instincts and intrinsic people skills. They can be spotted even when they are brand-new teachers and haven't even considered leadership for themselves. They stand out as individuals who instinctively consider solutions to unique problems, they take risks, and they are the ones who will stand and speak when no one else will.

I once worked with an assistant principal who'd found his way to school leadership for no other reason than he just felt he *should*. "It seemed like a logical next step," he told me. "My father was a high school principal, and it was sort of expected of me." He had been a fantastic teacher, beloved and respected by his students and colleagues alike. His reputation and lovable personality helped him land his first administrative job. Almost immediately, he seemed to wilt, both physically and emotionally. He worried all the time. He quickly gained a great deal of weight, managing stress by eating and adopting uncharacteristically sedentary habits. The job gnawed at him for many reasons. He hated being the "buck stops here" decision maker. He was anguished upon discovering that staff, students, and parents often grumbled about him behind his back. He dreaded and avoided difficult conversations. "I knew what skills I needed to be a principal, but it always felt forced. I never enjoyed it," he admitted. After a couple of years, he went back to the classroom, teaching in the same role he'd had before being an administrator. Just like that, he found his happiness. He felt successful again. "I'll finish my career right here in the classroom—where I belong," he says now.

He is a classic example of someone who *didn't* have an inherent instinct to lead and discovered—the hard way—that the principalship can't be forced. He couldn't begin to take care of himself when buried under the unmanageable stress of a job that clashed with his personality.

This is not to say that educators with inborn leadership characteristics find the job easy or anxiety-free. The difference is that successful principals gather energy and momentum from the challenges of the job.

With that said, the worst of days can tromp on us pretty heavily. When we are out of juice and feeling disenchanted, it helps to consciously consider ways to relax and enjoy the process, rediscover our purpose, and revive our souls.

Relax

Here's a truth: being a school principal shouldn't have the power to shake your world. It's not *that* special. After all, there are a *lot* of us doing this work, which gives us a lot of collegial support, should we seek it. That collegial tribe can help us remember that *everything is going to be all right*. It's not a flat and easy path, of course; we have our missteps and mistakes and our victories and triumphs. There are great days and horrible days. The job gives us fits and fatigue and, simultaneously, immeasurable pride and hope for our future.

Why, then, do so many of us get so worked up? Why do we let this job take away our composure and perspective?

I do it all the time. An issue will crop up that will set my hair on fire, and I'll zoom around like a madwoman trying to resolve the conflict, rework the schedule, communicate with stakeholders, rebuild a program—whatever it takes. Along the way, everything begins to feel monumental, and suddenly I'm acting, feeling, and reacting like I'm the president of the world, not just a little ol' principal of a little ol' school.

My shoulders will ache from tensing them in the anxious position. I have to double down on my efforts to *relax*. Here are a few things I try to remember in my efforts to chill out.

Remind yourself that the work always gets done. Really, it does. Maybe not on the time line we'd hoped for, and maybe not with flawless results, but it does get done. When overcome with a to-do list, it helps to remember that there's really only one thing we can do: chip away, smack on a good attitude, and keep going. In my office I have a large etching of the following statement: *Not to spoil the ending for you, but everything is going to be OK.* I read it often, forcing myself to really think about the words. And then I tell myself, "You know what? It really is."

Let go. Speaking of inspiring phrases, I have a beloved quote by Ralph Waldo Emerson on my cell phone case:

> Finish each day and be done with it. You have done what you could. Some blunders and absurdities have crept in; forget them as soon as you can. Tomorrow is a new day. You shall begin it serenely and with too high a spirit to be encumbered with your old nonsense.

Remembering this perspective offers reassurance that we can only do our best—and then, at day's end, we need to let it go. I've learned this the hard way, wasting untold hours worrying about things in the rearview mirror and bending my mind around things I could have, should have, would have done differently if I were just better, smarter, faster, wiser. *Pshaw,* I say now. Much better to tuck what I've learned in my back pocket, let go, and move on.

Remember the other things. Many principals find relief and satisfaction in doing something completely different than their daily work as a school principal. Not long ago, I led a principal forum in which we discussed other jobs or hobbies we were involved in. Those who had another activity to balance their education work were giddy about sharing it—what they loved about it and why it helped keep them balanced. The rest were, well, pretty jealous. Many vowed to find something else to fill them up beyond what happens within the walls of their schools. Here are the out-of-school activities, roles, and areas of interest the principals shared:

- Baking
- Ballroom, belly, or line dancing
- Bartending
- Carpentry
- Coaching
- DJing
- Farming and gardening
- Fitness instruction
- Local theater
- Ministry
- Musical performance
- Parenthood
- Photography
- Realty
- Retail
- Sales of various health and beauty products, oils, and clothing
- Styling
- Teaching as an adjunct professor
- Travel
- Travel agency
- Volunteering (women's shelters, food pantries, hospital service, or local community events such as festivals or parades)
- Working as an EMT
- Writing
- Yoga

Note that the items on this list do not include activities such as "Attending educational conferences" or "Reading professional books." None of them required additional hours at work. All helped take principals away from the depths of their school-based work and to an entirely new, refreshing way of thinking.

Here's another key point for those of us who are in the latter half of our careers. I've often heard retirees say it's important to foster other interests so that when a career comes to its inevitable end, a fresh set of interests is available to tap into. I don't want to be a worn-out retiree with no interests who depends on my children or my legacy to make me feel worthy. I've seen that happen too many times, and it terrifies me. Don't we want to have self-definition beyond the principalship? I think so.

Seek equanimity. I discovered the meaning of this word for the first time just a few years ago, which is a shame, because it is a *great* word and one I have since used frequently in my quest to lighten my "principal anxiety." To be in a state of equanimity is to have achieved mental calmness and composure, particularly when facing a difficult situation. The key words here, of course, are *mental calmness* —seeking space in our heads where we are at peace. If principals actively relax their minds, they launch relaxation of the body and spirit, too. For me, equanimity comes with deliberate breathing, yoga, and scheduled time alone. I know others who rely on solitary walks, meditation, guided imagery, consciousness-expansion work, spiritual and religious journeys, retreats with noneducator friends, and even focused, hands-on activities such as coloring, knitting, felting, or creating unique art.

Incidentally, I have found it counterproductive to adopt someone else's methodology for mindfulness. For me, following the rhetoric or teaching of a mindfulness guru leads directly to frustration or guilt. If I walk away still feeling burdened or anxious, I feel I have failed at some essential task, which makes me feel far worse than when I'd started. I believe we each need to develop our own definition of mindfulness, because it needs to come *from the mind that needs it.* In times of exhaustion, stress, and internal conflict, our minds tend to play tricks on us and distort our thinking. We need to learn to identify our *own* mind's faulty wiring first, and then we can address, manage, and dismiss it in a healthy way. If traditional mindfulness work isn't for you, find something that is—binge-watching a great TV series, taking a long walk with a podcast, going for a hard run with a heavy-metal playlist, playing with a dog. Whatever brings you peace and calm—that's *your* mindfulness.

Be you. I participated in an online forum about how principals manage their workload, and an innocent question quickly sparked a lively debate: "Do you go into the office during holiday breaks when the school is closed?" *Never,* said some principals. *I need the time to step away from the pressures of the job, reconnect with my home and family, and recharge my physical and emotional batteries.* Just as adamant was the other side: *Absolutely. I love to work when the school is empty. Without constant interruptions, I can get so much done. I catch up where I've fallen behind and prepare for what is coming up.* I'm in the latter camp, but I absolutely understand the former. There is no correct answer. We all work differently, and we all respond to stress differently. It's important to know thyself and take care of thyself accordingly.

Rediscover

A colleague of mine found herself in a professional rut. There was nothing specifically wrong. She'd empowered instructional leaders, so her teachers were doing great work in the classroom. Students were doing well on virtually all data and assessment measures. Parents were happy and comfortable, and students were active participants in the school's success. Everything seemed to be in good shape.

She was craving a project—something big, something that would matter to the world. She didn't want to just keep on keeping on; she wanted to use her skills and position to enhance and rediscover the reasons she'd become a principal in the first place. She took some time to watch, look, listen, and think about other needs her school might have, beyond typical expectations for student growth in academics. It was time, she decided, to use her school to give back—to itself.

Over the course of several months, she worked with her superintendent to develop partnerships with United Way, donation centers, and a local food pantry. She repurposed an underused classroom to make it into a "coat room." Families could come shop for various needs they might have—warm clothing, personal hygiene items, nonperishable foods, household goods and supplies. The pantry was open to anyone, no questions asked, maintained and beautifully organized by student and staff volunteers. It was a huge success, talked about and valued by her entire community. Neighboring schools learned about it and adopted similar programs. Reflecting on her project's triumphs, the principal told me, "I feel like I found a real need and worked to meet it. I was finally fulfilled—and so were the people who were part of our school community. It brought us closer together and improved my attitude toward my work."

There are other ways we might work to rediscover our purpose as principals of a school. Here are some ideas.

Jump on a super-cool committee—or start one. If the word *committee* or *meeting* strikes despair in your soul, you've probably served on too many frustrating, ineffective committees or attended way too many meetings. Can that mindset be flipped, though? If there is a unique or challenging bit of work that needs to be done, and if you can become part of something big and important, being in meetings isn't so painful. A friend of mine jumped on the committee tasked with completely overhauling our kindergarten assessments—a massive and potentially divisive undertaking. He threw himself into the work, learning all he could about early literacy and numeracy and connecting with district and state experts. In the end, he was a lot smarter than he'd been previously, students benefited from his enthusiasm and expertise, and he'd given himself a passion project to bolster his professional journey. I had this feeling myself when I worked on a committee to allocate money to staff who were interested in implementing significant innovation practices in their classrooms (see Chapter 4 for the details).

If something like this doesn't currently exist, why not launch something? Take on a problem, surround yourself with other smart and eager professionals, and lead the heck out of it.

Organize travel options for students. Spending time with students outside the typical learning environment can be surprisingly refreshing. If your school has travel opportunities for students, such as overnight "camping" trips for younger students or visits to major cities for older students, tagging along can be great fun. I've attended more than my share of trips to Washington, D.C., with middle schoolers, and recently I joined a group of teachers and 5th grade students who traveled to Boston for a five-day historical tour. Soon I'm hoping to go to Italy and Greece with some high schoolers. I thoroughly enjoy my time spent with students in an environment beyond the traditional classroom.

A colleague of mine says that early in his career he never joined student trips. "I was too busy—or thought I was too busy—managing things back at the building." Now, he says, "I never miss the chance to get out into the world with kids." Even if it is just a day trip or a traditional field trip, he says, "I have a great time being with the students, I get to help the teachers, and I always—*always!*—learn something new."

If programs such as these don't already exist at your school, why not be the catalyst or inspiration to begin one?

Immerse yourself in a student activity. I once worked as an assistant to a principal who adored athletics of all kinds, but though he enjoyed attending his middle school's sports events, he felt distant from the action. He missed the excitement and adrenaline that came from being a varsity coach, immersed with the players, but his district's policy prohibited him from being a paid coach. It didn't, however, prohibit him from volunteering. Talking one day to the head basketball coach at his district's high school, he wondered aloud if he could help in some way. The coach jumped at the chance to have him there, if only to help monitor playing time, break down film, and be a bonus set of eyes. It was a win-win: the coach and players benefited from the principal's experience and enthusiasm, and he got to be part of a team again.

Teach. I get great satisfaction in my work as an adjunct instructor in educational leadership at a local university. I love the preparatory reading, the planning, and overseeing a class of learners, most of whom are excited to be there. Doing so keeps my teaching skills sharp and helps ground me in the latest thinking and trends in education. Another benefit is that it helps me remember, all too well, the challenge of a large stack of papers to grade or occasional signs of student apathy. These are good reminders when I try to empathize with and relate to teachers.

If you're missing your teaching days, seek out nearby opportunities. Often, a local university will have openings for adjunct professors. If that's not a possibility, local or county educational service centers frequently seek practitioners and experts to launch or lead professional development classes.

Best of all, opportunities may be available right in your own backyard. How might your own school benefit from your experiences as a teacher? A colleague of mine is an enthusiastic writer. She started attending her school's "Power of the Pen" club meetings, writing with the students and offering to fill guest-teaching spots for the after-school club. The experience brought her back to her roots as a language arts teacher, helped her build important relationships with students, and gave her some street cred with teachers.

Lead a review of curricular resources. If teachers are using dated materials and resources, a great way to boost your self-confidence and energy might be to tap into your instructional roots by studying new resources and materials teachers can use in their classrooms. This work takes time and effort—forming committees, vetting vendors, securing funding—but it directly benefits students and boosts their learning experience, reenergizes teachers, and keeps you aware of what is being taught in a specific content area. You will find others are appreciative of your efforts and allocation of resources.

Rethink your workspace. Seriously, this is a great suggestion. I wholeheartedly believe in having an office space that makes one want to come to work. Even if the space is small, cold, and lined with many layers of paint covering cinder-block walls. Make it inviting. Incorporate lamps, rugs, some comfortable seating, pictures of students on the walls, and organized systems for task management. I don't have an eye for this sort of thing, but I have a couple of friends who do, so I happily rely on them to gussy up my workspace. I love the result, and it boosts my morale every time I come to work.

Update your résumé. Updating your résumé is actually great fun, and it doesn't need to be the first step in a job search. Instead, it can be the morale boost you need when you're feeling low. Just last winter I was pouty and sulky. It seemed everyone was grumpy with me. I couldn't think of a single thing I'd done right in weeks, and my self-efficacy was in the dumps. I decided to dust off and update my résumé. It was the last thing I wanted to do—a lot like pushing yourself to exercise when you'd rather lie on the couch for days. I forced myself to start anyway. Hours later, I looked up, having happily sunk deep into the process of self-examination and crafting complimentary phrases to describe myself. I felt so much better, reminded of how hard I'd been working—of the committees I'd served on, the initiatives I'd overseen, and the experiences I'd gained along the way. I found myself thinking, "Man, I'm really doing some good work here." It was the confidence builder I needed, just when I needed it.

Make a bold move. I was chatting with a former boss of mine, now happily retired, about this chapter of the book. "No need to write a whole chapter about rediscovering purpose," he said. "All anyone needs to do is change jobs."

"It's not that simple," I replied.

"It *is*, though," he said. "Each time I thought I'd reached the end of my professional rope, I threw myself into the challenge of getting a different job in a different school or district." He'd worked in three districts over the course of his career, holding principalships at the elementary, middle, and high school levels. All these moves were deliberate: he made them to rediscover his purpose and keep growing as a leader. Bold? Yes. Effective? Absolutely.

Revive

Let's end this book with a plea to bring joy and laughter back to the principalship.

I laugh a lot at work. I actively seek, and easily find, great humor in all kinds of things—a spot-on student retort, a well-executed prank between teachers, a careful plan gone awry in the most ridiculous way. There is a great temptation for principals to be overly serious—after all, we are educating children! What a noble and solemn responsibility! But I believe schools should be places where we have fun while we do our important work. That's why I am so proud of the culture of joy present in my school. Time and time again, visitors remark on the spirit of happiness they feel when they walk through the doors. "We can't describe it," they say. "It's just a *feeling*." Establishing this culture is a team effort, starting with the office staff. We all work to prioritize and promote this culture by offering heartfelt greetings, sharing positive stories, and capturing giggle-worthy anecdotes.

I love that I love going to work. With a job this taxing, I can't imagine *not* loving it. Here are suggestions for how to make your own commitment to a positive and happy workplace.

Spread happiness. I deliberately place opportunities for happiness wherever I can. We open staff meetings by asking someone to share an uplifting anecdote about a child—any child—or a short story about something that brightened the day. We remind staff how substitutes and visitors deeply appreciate a greeting and a smile when they pass in the hallways, the offer of a seat in the lounge, or help finding their way through the school building. I encourage thank-you notes and look for opportunities to provide a compliment or message of admiration. Throughout the day, I try to notice the funny, the amazing, the ridiculous, and the lovely. These things are everywhere in a school, and it would be a terrible shame not to take note of them.

Pass on the positivity. I often open meetings, trainings, group work, or even staff e-mail updates with a quick video or anecdote to start us off with a smile. No one likes a dour, grumpy leader. If I greet people with a grin and a lighthearted story, the whole mood in the school can shift and spread to others.

Model a good-natured attitude. I use self-deprecating humor a lot. Not long ago, I opened a staff meeting with a one-minute narrative about a really bad morning. I had been furious when mired in the situation, but a retrospective view made it quite funny. The staff got caught up in the story, undoubtedly because it was something they could all relate to, so we were all able to start our day with a good laugh. I didn't mind modeling humor at my own expense, because I'm showing others that it's healthy to laugh—especially at oneself.

Modeling an untroubled, perspective-based approach to our daily work really is the best way to make it happen. We can't run around the halls like the sky is falling and then snap at people to be calm and happy. We have to really live it, feel it, and pay it forward.

Foster an upbeat environment. We know that a work environment that includes play, creativity, and humor makes people more productive and effective. We know our students achieve more when they feel emotionally and socially engaged with their teachers and peers. We know positivity, laughter, and delight feed on themselves, and that people feel better when they are immersed in that kind of environment. What follows, then, is the simple truth that our whole school community will benefit if they enjoy days spent together.

Embrace the Eeyores. Every staff has its curmudgeons—people who find the negative, point out the mistakes, scowl and scoff from the back of the room. I once worked with a teacher who had an eagle eye for anything I did wrong. I used to set a timer to measure how long it would take her to reply to one of my e-mails with a correction.

I don't try to change those personalities. Quite the contrary. I accept them, give them a little good-natured ribbing if they don't mind, and let them be. If they are toxic, gossipy, or mean to kids, I'll address it. Otherwise I just remind myself that there is a place in the world for everyone, and the grouches certainly have a place in mine.

Sometimes I even find that my most Eeyore-type colleagues will begrudgingly have a good laugh every now and then—and will even, in a weak moment, admit that they appreciate a lighthearted approach to work. The negative fact-checker I once worked with? When I moved on from that school, she actually cried, and she has since sent me a note saying how much she misses me and the culture of happiness I insisted on. Who knew?

Ignore the impossible. We all have them: the staff members who seem intent on being miserable, who are only happy when they're unhappy. I remember a teacher I worked with—she always seemed to be grumpy and glaring, a permanent scowl on her face. Every single day, she would complain the whole way to her assigned bus duty, struggling with her coat and dropping some sort of passive-aggressive comment. One day I walked out with her and remarked on the miserable weather. "Yeah, no kidding," she snorted. "You should try being out here every day like *I* am, since *you* assigned me this duty *again* this year."

There were many things I wanted to say: "Actually, I *am* out here every day" or "Though I may have assigned this particular duty, you signed a contract agreeing to be part of duty assignments" or "We all have to pitch in, don't we?" What I most wanted to say was, "Can you please stop ruining the experience of everyone around you?" But I didn't say a thing.

I make a conscious decision not to let the impossibly impossible staff members affect me or bring me down. It is a choice, and I make it deliberately and with great effort. Sometimes I crack (see my venting strategy at the end of this section), but mostly I just shake my head, decide not to let it ruin my day, and move on.

Stay professional. It is important to note that all this light-hearted, find-the-joy stuff never crosses professional lines. Though I like to have fun, I am decidedly not running a comedy club. I just want people to feel upbeat and refreshed at work. We observe a few commonsense parameters. As a staff, we don't laugh at the expense of students. We don't make fun of others in a way that is inappropriate, hurtful, or offensive—ever. There's no need for such behavior; everyday life presents us with enough natural, harmless hilarity to eliminate the need for humor that is mean-spirited or damaging. Instead, we enjoy the mirth that exists all around us and amuse ourselves in just being human beings, surrounded by other human beings, all of whom have frailties and failures and celebrations and life wins.

Let it out. We all get grumpy occasionally, so we need times and places to vent. It wouldn't be healthy to be so Pollyanna-ish that no one can feel authentic or honest. When the negativity, frustration, and anger bubble up, we let it happen—and then move on. My assistant and I do this all the time: I'll go into her office, close the door, vent for a moment, and breathe deeply. She'll listen, smile, gently offer insight or perspective, and nudge me to move on. I do the same for her. We even joke about it. After indulging in a negative moment, we will remind each other, "Time to fix your face." We wipe away the scowl and replace it with a smile. We don't believe in stifling the crappy parts of our job, or the overwhelming frustration and exasperation we sometimes experience. We find it helpful to get it out and then put it firmly behind us.

● ● ●

Reviving the spirit of the principalship takes work, just as being in a good marriage or planning a good vacation does. When we consider the scope of a career, though, and how many hours we'll spend in this job over time, it is clear that the investment of time and energy devoted to the cause will pay off in untold ways. Certainly our students and staff will benefit from a leader who has energy, spirit, and a genuinely joyful attitude about the job, but so will we. It's a long and exhausting career. We might as well make it a long, exhausting, *fabulous* career.

References

Blad, E. (2018, April 10). Data: Schools have gotten safer over time. *Education Week*. Retrieved from https://www.edweek.org/ew/articles/2018/04/11/schools-have-gotten-safer-over-time.html

Cooper, H., Lindsay, J. J., Nye, B., & Greathouse, S. (1998). Relationships among attitudes about homework, amount of homework assigned and completed, and student achievement. *Journal of Educational Psychology, 90*(1), 70–83.

Hammond, Z. (2015). *Culturally responsive teaching and the brain: Promoting authentic engagement and rigor among culturally and linguistically diverse students.* Thousand Oaks, CA: Corwin.

Hattie, J. (2009). *Visible learning: A synthesis of over 800 meta-analyses relating to achievement.* New York: Routledge.

Horowitz, J. M., & Graf, N. (2019, February 20). Most U.S. teens see anxiety and depression as a major problem among their peers. Pew Research Center: Social & Demographic Trends. Retrieved from https://www.pewsocialtrends.org/2019/02/20/most-u-s-teens-see-anxiety-and-depression-as-a-major-problem-among-their-peers/

National Center for Education Statistics (NCES). (2018). Table 105.20. *Digest of education statistics.* Washington, DC: U.S. Department of Education, Institute of Education Sciences. Retrieved from https://nces.ed.gov/programs/digest/d17/tables/dt17_105.20.asp?current=yes

U.S. Census Bureau. (2018). *QuickFacts, United States.* Retrieved from https://www.census.gov/quickfacts/fact/table/US/IPE1202

Index

Page references followed by an italicized *f* indicate information contained in figures.

About the Author

Jen Schwanke has been an educator for more than 20 years, teaching or leading at all levels. She is the author of *You're the Principal! Now What? Strategies and Solutions for New School Leaders*, published by ASCD. She has written for *Choice Literacy, Education Week Teacher, Principal,* and *Principal Navigator* and presented at conferences for ASCD, as well as NAESP, Battelle for Kids, RRCNA, and various state and local education organizations. She has provided professional development to various districts in the areas of school climate, personnel, and instructional leadership. She is an instructor in educational administration at Miami University and has served on several state-level committees and workgroups focused on best practices in school leadership. She is currently a principal for the Dublin City School District in Dublin, Ohio. Follow her on Twitter @JenSchwanke.

Related ASCD Resources

At the time of publication, the following resources were available (ASCD stock numbers appear in parentheses).

Print Products

Becoming a Globally Competent School Leader by Ariel Tichnor-Wagner (#119011)

The Burnout Cure: Learning to Love Teaching Again by Chase Mielke (#119004)

The Coach Approach to School Leadership: Leading Teachers to Higher Levels of Effectiveness by Jessica Johnson, Shira Leibowitz, and Kathy Perret (#117025)

Coherent School Leadership: Forging Clarity from Complexity by Michael Fullan and Lyle Kirtman (#118040)

Committing to the Culture: How Leaders Can Create and Sustain Positive Schools by Steve Gruenert and Todd Whitaker (#119007)

Design Thinking for School Leaders: Five Roles and Mindsets That Ignite Positive Change by Alyssa Gallagher and Kami Thordarson (#118022)

Dream Team: A Practical Playbook to Help Innovative Educators Change Schools by Aaron Tait and Dave Faulkner (#119022)

Leading Change Together: Developing Educator Capacity Within Schools and Systems by Eleanor Drago-Severson and Jessica Blum-DeStefano (#117027)

Leading with Focus: Elevating the Essentials for School and District Improvement by Mike Schmoker (#116024)

Navigating the Principalship: Key Insights for New and Aspiring School Leaders by James P. Spillane and Rebecca Lowenhaupt (#118017)

Never Underestimate Your Teachers: Instructional Leadership for Excellence in Every Classroom by Robyn R. Jackson (#110028)

You're the Principal! Now What? Strategies and Solutions for New School Leaders by Jen Schwanke (#117003)

For up-to-date information about ASCD resources, go to www.ascd.org. You can search the complete archives of *Educational Leadership* at www.ascd.org/el.

PD Online

Leading Professional Learning: Building Capacity Through Teacher Leaders by Judy F. Carr (#PD13OC010S)

What Works in Schools: School Leadership in Action, 2nd Edition (#PD11OC119M)

ASCD myTeachSource®

Download resources from a professional learning platform with hundreds of research-based best practices and tools for your classroom at http://myteachsource.ascd.org/.

For more information, send an e-mail to member@ascd.org; call 1-800-933-2723 or 703-578-9600; send a fax to 703-575-5400; or write to Information Services, ASCD, 1703 N. Beauregard St., Alexandria, VA 22311-1714 USA.

The ASCD Whole Child approach is an effort to transition from a focus on narrowly defined academic achievement to one that promotes the long-term development and success of all children. Through this approach, ASCD supports educators, families, community members, and policymakers as they move from a vision about educating the whole child to sustainable, collaborative actions.

The Principal Reboot relates to the **safe**, **engaged**, **supported**, and **challenged** tenets.

For more about the ASCD Whole Child approach, visit **www.ascd.org/wholechild.**

WHOLE CHILD
TENETS

1 HEALTHY
Each student enters school healthy and learns about and practices a healthy lifestyle.

2 SAFE
Each student learns in an environment that is physically and emotionally safe for students and adults.

3 ENGAGED
Each student is actively engaged in learning and is connected to the school and broader community.

4 SUPPORTED
Each student has access to personalized learning and is supported by qualified, caring adults.

5 CHALLENGED
Each student is challenged academically and prepared for success in college or further study and for employment and participation in a global environment.